THE BATTLE OF LENS 1648

Condé beats the Spanish

Alberto Raul Esteban Ribas

'This is the Century of the Soldier', Fulvio Testi, Poet, 1641

HELION & COMPANY

Helion & Company Limited
Unit 8 Amherst Business Centre
Budbrooke Road
Warwick
CV34 5WE
England
Tel. 01926 499 619
Email: info@helion.co.uk
Website: www.helion.co.uk
X (formerly Twitter): @Helionbooks
Facebook: @HelionBooks
Visit our blog https://helionbooks.wordpress.com/

Published by Helion & Company 2025
Designed and typeset by Mary Woolley, Battlefield Design (www.battlefield-design.co.uk)
Cover designed by Paul Hewitt, Battlefield Design (www.battlefield-design.co.uk)

Text © Alberto Raul Esteban Ribas 2025
Illustrations as individually credited
Maps drawn by George Anderson © Helion & Company 2025
Colour artwork by Serge Shemenkov and Giorgio Albertini © Helion & Company

Illustrations attributed to Army Museum, Stockholm, are reproduced under the Creative Commons
license and derive from the web site, https://digitaltmuseum.se. Illustrations attributed to Royal
Armoury, Stockholm, or Skokloster Castle are reproduced under the Creative Commons license and
derive from the web site, http://emuseumplus.lsh.se. Other illustrations are reproduced under GNU
Free Documentation License (GNU FDL) coupled with the Creative Commons Attribution Share-
Alike License, or derive from the personal collections of the authors.

ISBN 978-1-804516-81-2

British Library Cataloguing-in-Publication Data.
A catalogue record for this book is available from the British Library.

For details of other military history titles published by Helion & Company Limited
contact the above address or visit our website: http://www.helion.co.uk.

We always welcome receiving book proposals from prospective authors.

Contents

1   The Franco-Spanish War   5
2   The Theatre of Operations of Flanders   6
3   The French Perspective   15
4   The Spanish Perspective   22
5   The Path Towards the Battle   28
6   The Battle   50
7   Repercussions   80
8   The Peace   120

Appendices:
I   Order of Battle of the French Army at the Battle of Lens,
      20 August 1648   123
II   Casualties in the French Army at the Battle of Lens,
      20 August 1648   126
III   Order of Battle of the Spanish Army at the Battle of Lens,
      20 August 1648   130
IV   Prisoners from the Spanish Army at the Battle of Lens   132

Bibliography   137

1

The Franco-Spanish War

In the words of François de Clermont, Marquis de Montglat, soldier, politician and historian of the reign of Louis XIV:

> The Swedish side was maintained by the actions of the Hertzog von Weimar and the *Maréchal* Horn, which, having lost the Battle of Nördlingen (1634), were the cause by which the Cardinal Richelieu encouraged the Most Christian King to declare war against the House of Habsburg. This great distraction gave the Swedes time to repair their loss; and the French, powerfully helping them, made The Emperor's cause into as bad a state as before.[1]

Engraving of the Battle of Nördlingen, 1634. Artist unknown. (Riksarkivet, Stockholm)

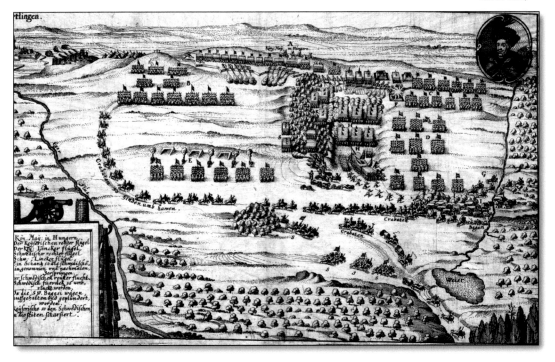

---

1   Marquis de Montglat, *Collection des Mémoires Relatifs à l'Histoire de France* (Paris: Foucault, 1826), p.93.

2

The Theatre of Operations of Flanders

The war between France and Spain continued throughout the whole reign of Philip IV and during his two decades as King he did not have a single year of peace. The war was provoked by the Imperial–Spanish victory at the Battle of Nördlingen (5–6 September 1634),[1] which forced the withdrawal of the Swedish-German army. France would support with cash, materiel and even the recruitment and paying of mercenaries, any enemy of Spain such as The Netherlands, Sweden, and even the Ottoman Empire,[2] but the victory of Nördlingen threatened a collapse of these powers and the revival of the Spanish power; because of which Richelieu was forced to a declaration of war between the two countries on 19 May 1635, under the pretext of Spanish aggression against the Bishopric of Trier, an ally of France. Spain's greatest fear had materialised, and to the fronts in the war of Flanders and Germany were now added Northern Italy, the Pyrenean Border and Southern Flanders.[3]

At the time, Ferdinand of Austria, known as the *Cardinal-Infante*, the younger brother of King Philip IV, was Governor General of the Spanish Netherlands. The Army of Flanders had to divide into two parts to defend the territory from a double-pronged attack. The French entered Flanders in 1635 with an army of 35,000 men under the command of *Maréchals* Urbain de Maillé, Marquis de Brézé, and Gaspard de Coligny, Duc de Châtillon. The Principe di Carignano, Tommaso Francesco di Savoia-Carignano, having assembled an army of 14,000 men faced off with the French on 20 May 1635 at the Battle of Avins, where the French lost 5,000 dead and the Spanish about 7,000. The Spanish had to retreat towards the centre of the country, leaving

---

1   For a detailed analysis of this battle see, Alberto Raúl Esteban Ribas, *The Battle of Nördlingen 1634* (Warwick: Helion & co., 2021) Century of the Soldier series, No.77.

2   For the international policy of Philip IV and his son Charles II see, Porfirio Sanz Camañes, *Tiempo de Cambios. Guerra, Diplomacia y Política Internacional de la Monarquía Hispánica (1648–1700)* (Madrid: Actas, 2013).

3   For more about the war between France and Spain in Flanders see, Alberto Raúl Esteban Ribas, *The Battle of Rocroi 1643* (Warwick: Helion & co., 2022) Century of the Soldier series, No.94; Davide Maffi, *En Defensa del Imperio. Los Ejércitos de Felipe IV y la guerra por la hegemonía europea (1635–1659)* (Madrid: Actas, 2014), pp.21–154.

The Battle of Nördlingen, attributed to Peter Snayers (1592–1667) and dated to 1634, oil on canvas. The perspective is from the rear of the Spanish lines. In the foreground, infantry companies in their stereotypical formation: musketeers and arquebusiers on the outside, and pikemen and Colours in the centre. Various cavalry squadrons can also be seen, mostly cuirassiers. In the background of the image, artillery pieces are shown on a hill; this is probably the Albuch Hill, where the main fighting of the day took place. (Nationalmuseum, Stockholm, NM 277)

the initiative to the French and the Dutch, who united their armies and besieged Leuven. It appeared that the campaign was going to be a success, but the Spanish cavalry harassed the French, hitting their supply lines, and forcing them to retreat towards France, while the Dutch continued to resist only with difficulty.

In 1636 Spain was determined to seize the strategic initiative; the Army of Flanders would remain on the defensive against The United Provinces, hoping that the Dutch would attack a town and thus focus their troops there and not invade the main territory; indeed, the Dutch besieged, and then captured the Fort of Schenkenschans on 30 April 1636.

Once the front had been stabilised against the Dutch, at the end of May, the *Cardinal-Infante* concentrated a powerful army to attack France: 1,600 cavalry and 6,000 infantry of the Army of Flanders, plus 8,000 cavalry and 9,500 infantry – Imperials, Lorrainers and from the Catholic League. The first action was the capture of La Capelle, which surrendered almost without a fight. The next towns to fall were Le Câtelet, Vervins, Bohain and Roye. At the beginning of August, the Spanish took Corbie, 100km from Paris; but their supply lines were too stretched, and a withdrawal was ordered. The Spanish captured Limburg from the Dutch on 16 October.

In 1637, France returned to the attack, attacking Alsace, Franche-Comté, Luxembourg and Picardy. And the Dutch besieged Breda, while the French captured Landrecies. The Spanish counter-attack allowed them to take Venlo on 25 August 1637, and Roermond on 5 September 1637, but they did not succeed in forcing Frederick Henry of Orange-Nassau to lift the siege of Breda, which finally surrendered on 11 October. In Luxembourg, *Maréchal* Châtillon took Dinant and Damvilliers, without Prince Tommaso Francesco being able to resist. And Franche-Comté was attacked by generals Longueville and Bernard of Saxe-Weimar.

The Netherlands had agreed to cooperate with France for the campaign of 1638 to take an important city of Flanders, and the objective was to be Antwerp. Because of this a campaign was planned for the two armies, under the orders of *Stadtholder* Frederick Henry and Willem van Nassau-Siegen to converge on the city. On 1 June, the French and the Dutch started their offensive from different borders of Flanders. Van Nassau-Siegen's army sailed down the Scheldt with the aim of taking the forts of Kallo and Verrebroek, and then seizing Blokkersdijk and Burcht in order to break the dikes and flood the countryside to prevent Antwerp's relief from the west, while the *Stadtholder* would attack from the north-west, occupying the suburb of Berchem to blockade Antwerp.

The Dutch attacked Kallo on 14 July, achieving their objectives. The *Cardinal-Infante* returned from the French border to take command of the operations in Antwerp, ordering that as many garrison troops as could be spared be added to his field force: on 20 July he had about 1,000 cavalry and 8,000 infantry, while van Nassau-Siegen had 300 cavalry and 6,000 infantry.

Portrait of Fernando *Cardinal-Infante* of Spain (1609–1641), from Guillielmus Becanus's *Serenissimi Principis Ferdinandi, Hispaniarum Infantis...*, engraved by Jacobus van Schoor and published in Antwerp by Johannes Meursius in 1636. King Felipe III, very religious, wanted his son Fernando to join the Catholic clergy, so at only 10 years old he was appointed Archbishop of Toledo and shortly afterwards was made a cardinal. Fernando was not ordained a priest, something not uncommon at that time when a member of royalty or the aristocracy held an ecclesiastical office. Fernando, like the entire Spanish Habsburg ruling family, was characterised by pale skin, blond hair and blue eyes, inherited from his predecessor Philip the Handsome of Flanders. The Archbishopric of Toledo was the richest Catholic diocese, after that of Rome. The Archbishop also claimed the Primacy of Spain, putting the primate above all other episcopal sees in Spain. (Metropolitan Museum of Art, New York. The Elisha Whittelsey Collection, Item 51.501.7407)

The Spanish launched simultaneous assaults against the outer defences of the forts of Kallo and Verrebroek, to prevent the Dutch from supporting and reinforcing each other. The action was successful and panic spread among the Dutch in the front line, which then spread to those in the forts, crowding into the boats to escape to the other side; the Spanish attacked, utterly routing the enemy. At least 3,000 Dutch were killed and many others taken prisoner; the Spanish lost fewer than 300 killed and about 800 wounded.

The *Stadtholder*'s army, with about 3,000 cavalry and 14,000 infantry, attempted to compensate for the defeat by besieging Gennep, advancing from Bergen op Zoom on 11 August and opening the siege on 14 August; Ferdinand assembled 12,000 men and marched to liberate the city and was joined en route by an Imperial army of about 6,000 men, under the command of Guillaume de Lamboy. In the face of this force the *Stadtholder* ordered a retreat and the threat, for 1638 at least, had been repulsed.

In the campaign of 1639, the Spanish-Imperial forces defeated the French at Thionville on 7 June. However, the French captured Hesdin on 29 June and the Spanish naval defeat at the Battle of the Dunes on 21 October gave supremacy at sea to the Dutch, aggravating the isolation of Flanders. Between 6,000 and 10,000 men, who would serve with the *Cardinal-Infante* in the campaign of 1640, and additionally several new Walloon tercios were recruited.

In 1640 the French prepared for a major campaign with an army of 8,000 cavalry, 24,000 infantry, and an artillery train of 50 pieces. While the Dutch would attack Dam and Bruges, a French army under the command of *Maréchal* de La Meilleraye would attack the line of the Meuse River, while *Maréchals* Chaulnes and Châtillon would attack Artois.

The Dutch launched their offensive at the end of May, threatening the area between Ghent and Bruges, but were defeated at Bruges and Hulst. The *Cardinal-Infante* then concentrated a field army of 6,000 cavalry and 16,000 infantry at Douai.

Meilleraye unsuccessfully besieged the strategic fortress of Charlemont, at the confluence of the Meuse and Givet rivers, and then moved to besiege Arras, since part of its garrison had been taken out to defend Saint-Omer, Béthune and Aire-sur-la-Lys. The French opened the siege of Arras on 13 June with an army of around 9,000 cavalry and 25,000

Francisco de Melo (1597–1651). Engraving by Pieter de Jode (II), dated between 1628 and 1670 (Rijksmuseum, Amsterdam)

EXCELLENTISSIMVS DOMINVS
D FRANCISCVS DE MELLO COMES DE AZVMAR.
GVBERNATOR BELGII ET BVRGVNDIÆ.

infantry. The city's defenders numbered 400 cavalry and 1,500 infantry under the command of the Irishman Owen Roe O'Neill. To relieve French pressure on Arras, the *Cardinal-Infante* harassed the French supply lines, but on 2 August, a convoy of 1,500 carriages, escorted by 2,000 men, managed to break through to bring supplies to the besiegers. It was therefore decided to attack the French siege lines, and on 3 August, several Spanish-Italian tercios attacked the French defences, which they managed to break, but not enough for the cavalry to penetrate through to the city. The attack ended with a Spanish retreat having taken 1,500 dead and wounded, to a loss of about 1,000 French.

On 8 August, O'Neill launched a sortie to halt the progress of the French trenches and mines, but it was repulsed and he was forced to offer the city's surrender the next day. The taking of Arras was Louis XIII's first great military success and was massively exploited by French propagandists.

The outbreak of the Catalan and Portuguese rebellions in 1640 caused Spanish action in Flanders to be relatively calm and the hopes of a Spanish offensive in Flanders in 1641 were cut short by the death of the *Cardinal-Infante* from smallpox. The Portuguese Francisco de Melo, loyal to the Spanish Crown, was appointed Governor.

Don Gaspar de Guzmán y Pimentel (1587–1645), Conde-Duque de Olivares and favourite (*valido*) of King Philip IV of Spain. Engraving made in 1778 by Francisco de Goya (1746–1828) after a portrait by Diego Velázquez (1599–1660). Olivares was descended from a minor branch of the powerful Medina-Sidonia family; his grandfather and father were both diplomats and military men. Olivares was born in Rome, where his father was, at the time, an ambassador. He came into contact with the Court when he was appointed gentleman entourage member (*gentilhombre*) of the young Prince Philip, the future Philip IV. From that point on, he won the Prince's friendship and intrigued to alienate other courtiers who also sought the favour of the future King. The figure of Olivares has always been surrounded by controversy: for some he was a prototype of a statesman, at the service of the King and the country, a tireless worker; for others, he was an opportunist, a despotic courtier who abused his office. In 1643 he resigned from his posts and retired to his estate in Loeches. (Metropolitan Museum of Art, New York. Item 31.31.15)

In the campaign of 1641, the French bet heavily on an offensive in Catalonia. The Spanish in response ordered offensive action in Flanders to try to relieve pressure on the Catalan front. Melo began the campaign by besieging the border town of Lens on 19 April 1642, it surrendered after two days. He then besieged La Bassée, which surrendered on 13 May, after 20 days of siege. France mobilised two armies to counter-attack: Henri de Lorraine-Harcourt, Compte d'Harcourt, advanced along the coast with 17,000 men, while Antoine III Agénor de Gramont-Toulonjon, *Maréchal* Guiche, marched towards Le Câtelet, with 3,000 cavalry and 7,000 infantry. Melo, with 6,000 cavalry and 13,000 infantry, informed about the size of both French armies, moved against Guiche, and on 26 May he deployed in battle on the plain in front of Honnecourt Abbey. The frontal assault of the Spanish infantry on the French trenches was thrown back, but the Spanish cavalry on the left flank, under the command of Jean de Beck, defeated the opposing French. The French cavalry on the right flank managed to break the line of the Walloon and Italian infantry, but was repulsed by a counter-attack. A new attack in the centre managed to definitively break the French defence, with more than 3,000 dead and about 3,400 prisoners. However, Melo decided not to continue his advance for fear of a French counter-attack.

The 1643 campaign in Flanders followed the same objective as that of the previous year – to relieve the pressure on Catalonia. Melo, after feinting with various possible objectives, reached the city of Rocroi.[4]

Louis de Bourbon, Duc d'Enghien, leading an army of 7,000 cavalry and 17,000 infantry, with 14 cannon, made a forced march to engage in battle. Melo, believing himself to be superior in both the number and the quality of his troops – he had about 6,000 cavalry, 17,000 infantry and 24 guns – allowed d'Enghien to enter the Rocroi plain, without harassing him. The battle of Rocroi, which was fought on 19 May, developed quite confusingly, and although French historiography wrote about it as a perfect stratagem devised by d'Enghien, the truth is that throughout the combat the French were repeatedly on the verge of collapse: but the lack of coordination between the Spanish infantry and the rest of the army, due to the passivity of the command of *Maestre de Campo General* Paul-Bernard de Fontaine, allowed the French cavalry charges to smash their Spanish opposition and attack the Walloon and Italian infantry from the flank, causing their withdrawal. The Spanish infantry was, finally, left alone on the battlefield, under attack by the entire French army, eventually forcing their surrender. The timely arrival of Jean de Beck's army, of 3,000 cavalry and 1,000 infantry, would have remedied the situation, but they arrived after the battle had ended, although rescuing the surviving units. The Spanish lost about 3,500 dead and almost 4,000 prisoners, while the French lost around 2,000 dead with the same number wounded.

---

4   For a detailed analysis of this battle, see Esteban Ribas, *Rocroi*.

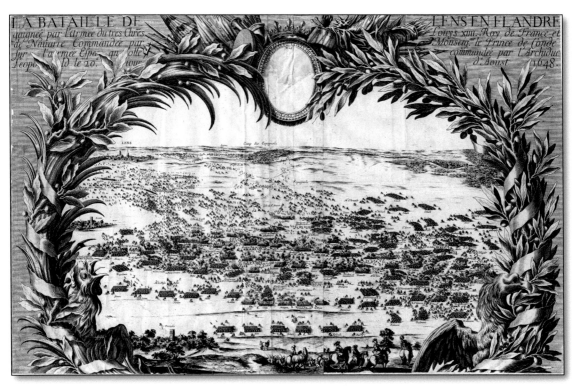

Contemporary engraving of the Battle of Rocroi in 1643, by François Collignon (c. 1610–87). This image of the battle is rather confusing: in the foreground are French soldiers escorting various supply waggons, looking towards the battle, which seems to be in its final stage: in the centre are the Spanish tercios still fighting although attacked from all sides. You can see the flanking movement of Gassion, and in the background a large number of Spanish soldiers are fleeing. (Riksarkivet, Stockholm)

The Spanish defeat at Rocroi was skilfully amplified by Mazarin, needing to consolidate the reign of Louis XIV, a minor under the regency of his Spanish Habsburg mother, Anne of Austria. Traditionally, it was at Rocroi that the myth of the invincibility of the Spanish tercios was destroyed. While it is unarguable that that the Spanish lost the battle, the Spanish Army did not sink into chaos. To the contrary, they quickly recovered and stopped the enemy advance, although they could not prevent the capture of Thionville on 10 August 1643. Furthermore, a Spanish contingent joined the Imperial-Bavarian army and defeated the Franco-German army at Tuttlingen on 24 November 1643,[5] inflicting on them more casualties than was suffered by the Spanish tercios at Rocroi.

Despite the defeats on other fronts, the enormous French population allowed various armies to be mobilised again which, in the case of Flanders, allowed them to launch various offensives that took several Flemish fortresses, with the intention of occupying the ports and stopping communication with Spain and the actions of the Walloon corsairs. In 1644, Gaston d'Orléans,

---

5   Esteban Ribas & Raúl, *La Batalla de Tuttlingen, 1643* (Madrid, Almena, 2014).

A view of the Spanish leaving Thionville on 10 August 1643, engraving by Jérôme David (before 1600 – after 1662). The city had been besieged by the French commanded by the Duc d'Enghien from 17 June to 10 August. Note the curious detail of how the Spanish soldiers are characterised – they all have the same face – and also notable is the difference in the fashion of moustaches between the Spanish and French – *cf* the illustrations of Melo and of the Duque de Alburquerque. (Public Domain)

Duc d'Orléans, took Gravelines on 19 July, after a bloody siege, and with the help of a Dutch fleet.

In the campaigns of 1645 and 1646, the French took Linken on 28 July 1645, Bourbourg on 7 August 1645, Mardyck on 26 August 1646, and Dunkirk on 12 October 1646. Pressure from the population of The United Provinces and from their economy forced the Dutch authorities to enter into peace negotiations with Spain, within the framework of the peace talks to end the Thirty Years' War. The United Provinces wanted a conclusion to the war of independence that had already lasted for 80 years but, additionally, they were afraid of the rise of France as a result of the exhaustion of Spain by having a war on two fronts.[6]

Furthermore, the progress of the war in recent years had been a balance between Spain and The United Provinces and neither saw it as a realistic option to return to the *status quo ante bellum* of 1568. All of which motivated The United Provinces and Spain to conclude a separate peace, and the Treaty

---

6   To understand the Spanish-Dutch approach see Peter H. Wilson: *Europe's Tragedy: A New History of the Thirty Years' War* (London: Penguin, 2010), pp.503–506.

of Münster of 30 January 1648 finally recognised the independence of The United Provinces.[7]

With the *de jure* recognition of the independence of The United Provinces – although this independence had been *de facto* for several decades – Spain also recognised the territorial limits of the new state, and sovereignty over a significant number of territories captured during the war, both on the European Continent as well as in the East and West Indies. The peace treaty also further cemented the foundations of the economic boom of The United Provinces.

Spain finally signed a peace with The United Provinces because, after so many decades of war, it was forced to choose between failing against France or against The United Provinces. If Philip IV wanted to suppress the Portuguese and Catalan rebellions and continue the war against France with a chance of success, he could not afford to continue the war against the Dutch. Consequently, Spain was finally forced to renounce its claims over Netherlands territory and Spain also had to make important concessions in commercial matters, such as with regards to trade with the east and territorial expansion in some areas of America.

Peace with The United Provinces allowed Spain to concentrate its efforts in Flanders on a single front in the war, and thus freeing men and money to focus on the war against France. Spain was, however, still simultaneously fighting the rebellions in Portugal and Catalonia, which had broken out in 1640,[8] and in 1647 a revolt also broke out in Sicily and Naples.[9]

---

7   Martin A. Galán, *La Paz de Westfalia (1648) y el Nuevo Orden Internacional* (Badajoz: Universidad de Extremadura, 2015), pp.3–15; Montglat, *Collection des Mémoires*, p.93.

8   See J. H Elliott, *The Revolt of the Catalans: In Study in the Decline of Spain (1598–1640)*, (Cambridge: CUP, 1984).

9   Peter H. Wilson: *Europe's Tragedy: A New History of the Thirty Years' War* (London: Penguin, 2010), pp.501–503, covers the Neapolitan revolt in greater detail.

3

The French Perspective

The loss of Lens in 1647, taken by *Maréchal de France* Jean de Gassion, had been a severe setback for Spanish Flanders, since it was an important city, well-fortified, and a city that covered the south of the Spanish Netherlands, being a communications hub between Arras, Calais, Lille and Cambrai. After the city's fall, Mazarin ordered the Marquis de Villequier and the *ingénieur* Langre to have the city's defences demolished, to limit the strategic importance of this city in the future and prevent, if the Spaniards recovered it, its use to threaten French territory.

In previous campaigns, the French had occupied a large part of the Spanish territory. In the province of Flanders, the cities of Gravelines, Mardyck, Dunkirk, Bergues, Furnes, Courtrai, Saint-Venant, Bolduque, Linguen as well as other minor towns; in Artois, the cities of Arras, Béthune, Baupame, Hesdin, Lens and La Bassée; and in Luxembourg, Thionville and Damvillers had all been lost by Spain.[1]

The war against Spain had moments that were favourable to the French and others that were not. The Catalan campaign of 1647 was led by Duc Louis II de Bourbon, who after the death of his father Henri II de Bourbon-Condé on 26 December 1646, inherited the title of Prince de Condé, under which title he would be become famous. In Catalonia, Condé led his army to reconquer Lerida: a doubly emblematic place, since Philip IV had sworn there, in 1644, to the constitution of Catalonia after it having been reincorporated into the Spanish Monarchy and, furthermore, it was the key defensive position of the west of the Principality of Catalonia. However, Condé failed against the fierce defence led by the Spanish General Gregorio Brito y João.

After his relief of the generalship in Catalonia, Condé headed to his lands in Dijon in Burgundy; he did not wish to return to Paris, with its palace intrigues, the conflict between the nobility

Jean de Gassion (1609–1648). Portrait by an anonymous artist-engraver, dated to between 1639 and 1668. (Rijksmuseum, Amsterdam)

---

1   Alonso Pérez de Vivero Y Menchaca, Conde de Fuensaldaña: 'Relación de lo Sucedido en Flandes desde 1648 a 1653' in *Colección de Documentos Inéditos para la Historia de España* [CODOIN], tome 75 (Madrid|: Miguel Ginesta, 1880), p.549.

Portrait of Cardinal Richelieu (1585–1642), engraving by Claude Mellan (1598–1688), published in Paris by Sebastien Cramoisy in 1651. He was ordained a bishop in 1607 at the age of 22, entered politics and was appointed *Ministre des Affaires Étrangères* (Minister of Foreign Affairs) in 1616, made a Cardinal in 1622, and *Principal Ministre d'État* (Principal Minister of State, 'prime minister') of Louis XIII in 1624. As *Principal Ministre d'État* of France, he consolidated the monarchy by combating the internal factions, countering the power of the nobility, and he turned France into a strongly centralised state. Its foreign policy, on the other hand, focused on countering the power of the Austro-Spanish Habsburg dynasty. (Metropolitan Museum of Art, New York. Item 41.57.36)

and the Regent, much less meet Mazarin, whom he blamed for denying him the resources necessary for his campaign in Catalonia.[2]

During the autumn of 1647, Louis XIV, aged only 9, had fallen ill with smallpox and he almost died; his brother, Philip, Duc d'Anjou, had also been ill and France had been very close to a succession crisis.[3]

Given the illness of the young Princes, the French Court was aware of the movements of the other two possible claimants to the throne: the King's uncle, the conspirator Gaston d'Orléans, Duc d'Orléans, and his distant cousin, the Prince de Condé.

Gaston watched Condé's return to Paris with concern as he knew that the young general had much more approval with the people and the nobility; and although d'Orléans considered himself the natural heir if his two nephews died, he feared that his poor reputation – not in vain had he repeatedly conspired against his brother Louis XIII – would cause him to be rejected at Court. Condé knew he was being watched both by the Regent/Mazarin faction and also by d'Orléans and his sycophants.

---

2   Eveline Godley, *The Great Condé: A Life of Louis II De Bourbon, Prince of Condé*, (London: John Murray, 1915), p.196.
3   Godley, *The Great Condé*, p.198.

The courtiers watched the movements of the two possible claimants, and although some took a stand in favour of one or the other, the majority did not want to take a side for fear of reprisals from Mazarin. In any case, the different characters of d'Orléans and Condé were revealed: d'Orléans did not hide his aspiration to be Regent for his nephew if he remained ill, since he assumed that, given the rejection that the Queen's/Mazarin's regency government had aroused, if his nephew's illness lasted his supporters would offer him the regency. He even dreamed that he could possibly become King if the King and his brother died. By contrast, Condé was much more cautious and reserved. He knew that, despite his prestige, he did not have much support among the nobility. Furthermore, his campaign in Catalonia had not gone well: the failure of the Lerida campaign at the time eclipsed the impressive triumphs achieved in the Battles of Rocroi, Freiburg and Nördlingen. In any case, faced with d'Orléans' petulance, Condé, blessed with a great intelligence, opted for discretion and to focus on military and not political issues.[4]

The Battle of Rocroi, contemporary engraving. The engraving is as much about the figure of the Duc d'Enghien, who stands out across the front of the picture, as it is about the battle. The cuirassiers around d'Enghien may be representative of his lifeguard or of a company of *gendarmes*. Note the accurately depicted Standards which does indicate, perhaps, the reliability of the rest of the illustration although d'Enghien's lack of a helmet is almost certainly artistic licence to better depict the 'hero' of the scene. (Stephen Ede-Borrett collection)

---

4   Godley, *The Great Condé*, p.198.

For this reason, Condé did not take part in the conflict that arose between d'Orléans and the Queen over the appointment of the Abbé de La Riviére, d'Orléans' protégé and confidante, as minister of state. Mazarin did not want Riviére as either minister or a Cardinal. D'Orléans, however, brought his influence to bear and succeeded in getting the Queen and Mazarin to give in to the appointment.[5]

By early 1648, the beginning of a conflict between the Crown of France and the nobility was already looming. During the preceding months, unrest had been growing, both among the nobility – because of the power of the Regent and her *Principal Ministre d'État* – and among the people, because of the high tax burden from the expense of the war. Spain, whose global empire gave it the resources to defend its vast and distant possessions, even though it had a war on so many open fronts (Flanders, Italy, North Africa, America and Asia), had been at war for a century. France, by contrast, was now unable to keep up the pace of the war, even though it had been at war for only a decade.

The superintendent of finances, Michel Particelli d'Emery, was an

Louis de Bourbon, Prince de Condé (1621–1686). Condé participated in the victory of the Battle of Valenciennes against the French on 16 July 1656, as well as at the Battle of the Dunes on 14 June 1658, won by Turenne. After the Peace of the Pyrenees of 1659, he was pardoned by Louis XIV and thereafter fought against Spanish, Dutch and Imperial forces (Condé Museum, PE 131) Portrait by Pieter Huybrechts, between 1635 and 1653 (Rijksmuseum, Amsterdam)

unpopular, and corrupt man, encouraged by Mazarin to obtain resources in any way he could. Venality in office was the order of the day, and many funds did not find their way into the royal coffers, but into Particelli's. Meanwhile, the people suffered and the troops received neither the money nor the sustenance necessary to keep them on campaign. When, in January 1648, Particelli reinstated a tax on all house property on the outskirts of Paris, the inhabitants of the Saint-Denis district complained to *Parlement*, which set up a commission to appear before the Regent, who was infuriated by their haughty attitude, even though they were merely defending the rights of the citizens. In the Privy Council, most of the ministers advised the Regent and Mazarin to give in to the *Parlement*'s pressure and to ease the tax burden. In such a heated atmosphere, as spring approached Mazarin concluded that a military triumph was needed to address the situation, or the regency would fall.[6]

Condé lived in Paris and kept a low profile, aloof from public life, but he let the Regent know that he could count on his support, as he did not want to be at odds with her or with Mazarin. In fact, the pressure of events forced Mazarin to seek Condé's support: reasons of state compelled the Cardinal to call on a general of prestige to defend the country against a threat from the Spanish Army of Flanders. Henri de La Tour d'Auvergne, Vicomte de Turenne, was indispensable to defend the German front, and Jean de Gassion and Josias Rantzau were ruled out because of their failures against the Spaniards and the

---

5   Montglat, *Collection des Mémoires*, pp.85–87.
6   Godley, *The Great Condé*, p.200.

Imperials.[7] However much it weighed on Mazarin, he had to rely on Condé's help. The new military assignment as supreme commander of a new French army was a very tempting rank to Condé's ego; Mazarin knew it was a sweet the Prince would want to savour, and from this new command position, the Cardinal could keep Condé 'in check', whereas, if left behind, the Cardinal feared Condé would intrigue against him.[8]

Condé's appointment to command the army in the campaign against Flanders thus meant a reconciliation with the Regent and the Cardinal, to their mutual benefit: Mazarin needed to regain the prestige and confidence of the French nation and secure his power vis-à-vis the nobility, and a military success for Condé would be the perfect rubric.[9] Condé needed to be accepted by the two people ruling France, to be reassured against the palace intrigues and to show that the Regent and the Cardinal could trust him, that he posed no threat.[10]

Cardinal Mazarin, Ministre d'Anne d'Autriche et de Louis XIV (1602–1661). Engraving by Jean Morin (c. 1605–1650), after Philippe de Champaigne (1602–1674). Mazarin's life was a succession of adventures that did not presage that he would devote himself to either a religious life or to French politics; as a young man he was very studious, but also an inveterate gambler. Initially he was to be a lawyer or a military officer, but Pope Urban VIII took notice of him and entrusted him with diplomatic posts, which he carried out with great skill. He was sent to Paris as an ambassador, where he developed a good working relationship with Richelieu: he became the French agent in Rome and finally in 1638 Richelieu succeeded in having him appointed cardinal and settled permanently in France. He became a protégé of Richelieu, whom he succeeded in 1642. However, Mazarin's succession to the post of *Principal Ministre d'État* to Louis XIII was neither automatic nor immediate, and it was the Regent Anne who appointed him *Principal Ministre d'État* and head of the government, after getting rid of his rivals De Noyers and De Chavigny. (Collection of the Metropolitan Museum, New York. Item 41.56.13)

---

7   Aumale indicates that Mazarin initially intended to send Turenne to Flanders for the 1648 campaign, but events in Germany, with the Imperial advance, made his presence in Germany indispensable (Aumale, *Histoire des Princes de Condé*, p.187).

8   Wilson: *Europe's Tragedy*, p.506.

9   Wilson: *Europe's Tragedy*, p.506.

10   Godley, *The Great Condé*, p.198.

His brilliant military record made him particularly suited to defending northern France and attacking Flanders – unlike when he had been appointed commanding general in 1643, with virtually no military experience – and his youth, arrogance, elegance and membership of the high nobility gave him the necessary prestige and respect among the nobility, the military hierarchy, and the people, who urgently needed a hero who they could trust to raise the country's morale.

Although France was maintaining armies in Germany, Italy and Catalonia, at a huge expense, Mazarin desperately needed a triumph and that assured Condé that Mazarin would not skimp on efforts to ensure that the army had the resources necessary for the upcoming campaign.[11]

Condé left for his new command in mid-April, and set up his headquarters in Arras, from where he planned the campaign. There he concentrated the four regiments that had accompanied him in Catalonia (the *Régiments de Condé, Conti, Anguien, Persan*).[12] The first step in his plan was to attack Ypres; this objective was not chosen by Condé, but followed Mazarin's directive, which were based on a Rantzau's ideas.[13] Rantzau himself, from Dunkirk, and *Lieutenant Général* Philippe de Clérambault, Compte de Palluau, from Courtrai – where he had 4,000 men at his disposal[14] - would converge on Ypres and take it by assault. On paper, it was a simple and effective idea, but the reality could be different.[15]

So Condé thought, who expressed his misgivings about the plan in a letter to Mazarin.[16] The forces of Rantzau and Palluau were not sufficient to take the city by storm and too small to undertake a siege. Condé informed the Cardinal that he had instructed Palluau to make a thorough reconnaissance of Ypres and its defences and that, if a *coup de main* was feasible, he would support him. However, if Ypres had to be besieged, he would not authorise such a move, Condé's main force would first have to move into the area.[17]

In any case, the mere fact of advancing troops eastwards was already a great risk, since the Spanish controlled the cities of Lille, Tournai and Oudenarde. According to French estimates, the Spanish Governor, Archduke Leopold Wilhelm, had 25,000 troops at his disposal: around 7,000 cavalry and 14,000 infantry and 3,000 Lorrainers troops, (11 German regiments, 6 Spanish tercios, 3 Walloon tercios, 3 Italian tercios, 2 English regiments, 1 Irish and 1 Burgundian tercios); in addition, 11 Walloon regiments and 260 companies guarded the main towns.[18] Over the next few days, Condé and

---

11 Godley, *The Great Condé*, p.204.
12 Aumale, *Histoire des Princes de Condé*, p.189.
13 Aumale describes Rantzau as a general with courage but little else, with little intelligence; it is clear from his words that Condé had little regard for the German general, nor did he have any sympathy for Palluau (Aumale, *Histoire des Princes de Condé*, pp.189–191).
14 Hardy, *Batailles Françaises*, p.100.
15 Godley, *The Great Condé*, p.202.
16 Aumale, *Histoire des Princes de Condé*, p.191.
17 According to Aumale, Palluau misrepresented certain information for his own convenience, in order to absolve himself of responsibility for subsequent events, claiming that he had alerted Condé to the risks of the action on Ypres and Courtrai (Aumale, *Histoire des Princes de Condé*, p.193).
18 Aumale, *Histoire des Princes de Condé*, p.192.

Palluau corresponded intensely on the initial idea of a surprise attack on Ypres. Condé was not convinced and rejected the operation.[19]

Aerial view of modern-day Lille. For centuries, the city was part of the County of Flanders, then of the Duchy of Burgundy and later was a part of the Spanish Netherlands. During the numerous wars between France and Spain, the city was besieged many times. With the Peace Treaty of Aix-la-Chapelle of 1668, it finally passed into the hands of France. In just three years, under the supervision of Vauban, France built an imposing defensive system of singular beauty, and it became known by the nickname 'Queen of Citadels'. Today it is a historical-sports complex, surrounded by a beautiful forest. (Google maps)

19   Godley, *The Great Condé*, p.203.

4

The Spanish Perspective

From 1647, the Governor of the Spanish Netherlands and Commander in Chief of the Spanish forces was Archduke Leopold Wilhelm[1] of Austria, brother of The Emperor Ferdinand III.[2] Philip IV had agreed to his cousin Leopold taking over the government of Flanders for several reasons. Firstly, the Archduke's princely rank gave him enormous prestige with the Spanish generals in Flanders, and meant that they could not question his authority; secondly, Philip IV wanted greater involvement of The Empire in the war in Flanders, although Emperor Ferdinand was too busy fighting the Swedes, the German Protestants and the French to be able to send many men to Flanders. However, Philip IV believed that if The Emperor's younger brother was in charge of the Government of Flanders, The Emperor would not leave his brother unsupported, and would send him resources and troops so that he would retain his position and avoid defeat and humiliation.

The Archduke began his public life in 1626 as Bishop of Passau and Strasbourg and Prince Abbot of the monastery of Murbach. His brother The Emperor Ferdinand III gave him supreme command of the Imperial Army from September 1639 to February 1643. He succeeded in driving back the Swedes, but was defeated at the second Battle of Breitenfeld on 2 November 1642. He led the Imperial army again from May 1645 until the end of the year.

In 1646 Philip IV offered the Archduke the post of Governor of the Spanish Netherlands, which he accepted, and he was the representative of the King of Spain in the negotiations for peace with The United Provinces.

On 8 March 1648 the new *Gobernador General de las Armas de Flandes* (Governor General of the Armies of Flanders), Alonso Pérez de Vivero y Menchaca, Conde de Fuensaldaña, arrived in the port of Ostend, and also held the post of *Superintendente de la Hacienda* (Superintendent of the

---

1   R. Vermeir, 'Un Austriaco en Flandes. El Archiduque Leopoldo Guillermo, Gobernador General de los Países Bajos meridionales (1647–1656)' in *La Dinastía de los Austria: las relaciones entre la Monarquía Católica y el Imperio* (Madrid: Ediciones Polifemo, 2011), Volume 1, pp.583–608
2   Godley, *The Great Condé*, p.203.

Archduke Leopold Wilhelm of Austria (1614–1662). Portrait by Cornelius Galle (II), between 1638 and 1678. The Archduke wears the Spanish fashion of moustache and goatee, but also shows the French fashion of wearing long hair – both traits with which he is depicted in other engravings and on his portraits. He is depicted in black three-quarter armour; and the scarf he is wearing would have been red, the identifier of Spanish and Imperial soldiery. (Rijksmuseum, Amsterdam)

Treasury).[3] Fuensaldaña had gone to Flanders as a member of the entourage (*gentilhombre*) of *Cardinal-Infante* Fernando of Austria and in 1632 was appointed captain of an infantry company. Over the following years he rose through the military ranks: *castilian* (military governor) of Cambrai in February 1635; in 1636 he was appointed *maestre de campo*, the colonel's rank in a Spanish tercio; in April 1640 he was promoted to *General de la Artillería del Ejército de la Frontera de Francia* (General of Artillery of the Army of the Frontier of France); then in 1641 he was promoted *General de la Caballería del Ejército de la Frontera de Holanda* (General of Cavalry of the Army of the Frontier of Holland). In 1643, he was promoted to *Maestre de Campo General del Ejército de la Frontera de Holanda* (Field Master General of the Army of the Dutch Frontier); in 1644, he was made *General de la Caballería del Ejército de la Frontera de Francia* (General of the Cavalry of the Army of the French Frontier). In 1646, he left Flanders for his new post as *Gobernador*

---

3   Anonymous, Biblioteca Nacional Hispánica, Mss. 2379, 'Sucesos de año 1648', f.79; Pérez, 'Relación de lo Sucedido', p.549.

Jean de Beck (1588–1648), engraving by Franciscus de Nÿs. This general perfectly embodies the social advancement that a career in Arms could generate. From a humble family, enlisting as a simple soldier, he climbed the military ranks in the Spanish and Imperial Armies. He enlisted as a simple soldier in the Imperial army in 1619 and by 1633 was a subordinate general in Wallenstein's army. In 1635 he returned to Luxembourg where he joined the garrison, and he served in the Spanish Army in Flanders thereafter, taking part in all of the actions of the war against France. He was ennobled by The Emperor and by the King of Spain as a reward for his excellent service record. (Public Domain)

de las Armas de Extremadura (Governor of the Army of Extremadura) for the war against the Portuguese rebels.

On his new arrival to Flanders, Fuensaldaña prepared the next campaign and listed the main places in French hands: in Flanders, the towns of Gravelines, Mardyck, Dunkirk, Bergues, Furnes, Courtrai, Saint-Venant; in Artois, the towns of Arras, Béthune, Baupame, Hesdin, Lillers, Lille, La Bassée; in Luxembourg, Thionville and Damvillers.[4]

The Spanish general staff in Flanders was an excellent example of the amalgam of territories in Philip IV's empire: Spanish noblemen, such as the Conde de Fuensaldaña; Walloon noblemen, such as the Prince of Ligne, the Prince of Salm and the Count of Bucquoy; Italian noblemen, such as Marchese Sfondrato; German mercenaries, such as the Graf von Beck; and Lorraine allies, such as Ligniville and Clinchamp.

The Army of Flanders' general staff was:

Captain General and Governor of Flanders: Archduke Leopold Wilhelm of Habsburg

Governor General of the Army of Flanders: Conde de Fuensaldaña

General Field Master: Jean de Beck

General of the Cavalry of Flanders: Charles Albert de Longueval, Count of Bucquoy and Gratzen, Baron of Vaulx

Lieutenant General of the Cavalry of the Dutch Border, Juan Maria de Borja y Aragón, 9th Duque Consort de Nájera, 7th Marqués de Cañete

Lieutenant General of the Cavalry of the French Border, Pedro de Villamor y López Zatón

---

4   BNH, Mss. 2379, 'Sucesos', f.79; Pérez, 'Relación de lo Sucedido', pp.549–550.

Alonso Pérez de Vivero y Menchaca, Count of Fuensaldaña (1603–1661). Portrait by Cornelius Galle (II), between 1638 and 1678 (Rijksmuseum, Amsterdam)

The theoretical strength of the Army for the campaign was 34,000 men,[5] but the reality was very different. When Archduke Leopold concentrated his forces in Lille, he had only 21,000[6] to 25,000 men,[7] including 7,000 cavalry, and 38 guns. There were 32 infantry regiments or *tercios* – 5 from Lorraine, 11 from Germany, 6 from Spain, 3 from Wallonia, 3 from Italy, 2 from England, 1 from Ireland, 1 from Burgundy-Franche-Comté.

The infantry was composed of 10 different nationalities![8]

---

5   BNH, Mss. 2379, 'Sucesos', f.79.

6   Hardy, Batailles Françaises, p.101.

7   Godley, *The Great Condé*, p.204.

8   In his account of the Battle of Lens, Aumale describes how the Spanish infantry had been slow to adapt to the new style of warfare -he refers, no doubt, to the stereotype that the tercios formed into rigid formations, bristling with pikes, like a Macedonian phalanx. Furthermore, he argues that a weakness of the Spanish Army was the plurality of the nationalities of its troops:

The infantry is in question: all these small battalions are more manoeuvrable; but will they have the solidity of the phalanx of the 'dark-skinned men' (*hommes basanés*) of those 'old tercios' that will never be seen again? The confusion of languages and origins is greater than ever: in the 10 battalions that form the front line of the centre, there are

This matchlock musket in the Deutschlandmuseum dates to the late sixteenth century and was very probably still in use during the Thirty Years' War. Then as now, well-maintained weapons were used over several generations. The weapon has an overall length of 157cm with a barrel length of 122cm. The musket fired an 18mm ball, which was fairly usual for muskets of the time. The maker is unknown, but a mark on the barrel resembles a crown.
(https://www.deutschlandmuseum.de/en/collection/matchlock-musket)

Among the native Spanish units present in Flanders, the following can be confirmed: the Tercios of Solis, Bonifaz, and Vargas (Spanish). There were also some companies of native Spanish cavalry, which were organised independently.

The Walloon infantry stood out for their numbers and quality: the Tercio of La Motte (*Maestre de Campo* Lancelot de Grobbendonck, Baron de Wezemaal); the Tercio of Bucquoy (*Maestre de Campo* Albert François de Croy, Conde de Meghen); the Tercio of Barbençon (*Maestre de Campo* Jacques Cottrel and Conde de Bois de Lessines); the Tercio of Cocqhove (*Maestre de Campo* Philippe-Charles Spinola, Barón d'Andres and Conde de Bruay); The Tercio of Baucignies (*Maestre de Campo* George-Jean de Thiennes, Barón de Brouck); The Tercio of Conteville (*Maestre de Campo* Philippe de Lannoy, Lord of Conteville and Conde de la Motterie); the Tercio of Trazegnies (*Maestre de Campo* Philippe d'Anneux, Barón de Crèvecoeur and Conde de Wargnies); the Tercio of Croy (*Maestre de Campo* Eustache de Croy, Conde de Roeulx); the Tercio of Stoppelaar (*Maestre de Campo* Frans Stoppelaar); the Tercio of Molin (*Maestre de Campo* Jean Molin d'Hernani); the Tercio of Gammerages (*Maestre de Campo* Alexander Richardot-Grusset, Conde de Gammerages and Principe de Steenhuise).

The Italian units consisted of Avalos' Tercio (*Maestre de Campo* Giovanni delli Ponti), Spinelli's Tercio (*Maestre de Campo* Giovanni Battista Molini), Baglioni's Tercio (*Maestre de Campo* Carlo Campi), Guasco's Tercio (*Maestre de Campo* Giuseppe Guasco). In addition, there were English volunteers in Parham's regiment (Colonel Henry Norris) and Murphy's regiment (Colonel Shane Murphy), and 2 Irish Tercios of Marais and Plunkett.

---

three Lorrainer, two Walloon, two Irish, one German, one Italian, and only one Spanish. It is this last element, the solid element par excellence, which is no longer found in equal proportion: only three former battalions of 'native Spaniards' placed in the second line with three others of various nationalities. Aumale, *Histoire des Princes de Condé*, p.234.
To counter these claims that Spanish tactics were outdated see Maffi, *En Defensa del Imperio*, pp.199–204.

There were various types of cavalry: *Bandes d'Ordonnance* (feudal nobility cavalry) which were barely effective; various companies of '*Gardes du Corps*' of the authorities (the Governor, *Maestre de Campo General*); companies of light cavalry, most especially the Croatian units, and German cuirassiers. Additionally these were augmented by the cavalry of the Duc de Lorraine – the *Chevau-Légers* of Lorraine were considered the best in Europe.[9]

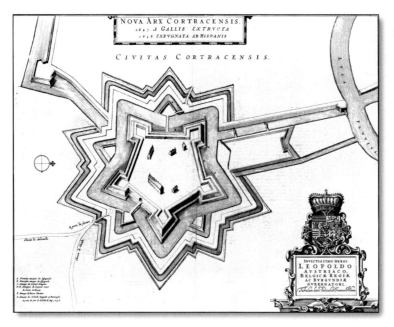

The Fortifications of Courtrai in the late 1640s. (Riksarkivet, Stockholm)

The Spaniards were aware that the French field army might number more than 30,000 troops; fearing that, if they were to be assembled, they could unleash an offensive that would break the defence of Flanders, the Archduke asked the Duc de Lorraine to send part of his army quickly to join the defence of Flanders. However, Duc Charles IV did not agree, and delayed sending the troops. When they did arrive and joined the Army of Flanders, it was considered too late to launch an offensive before the French did.[10] Precious time had been lost...

Spanish spies reported that the Prince of Condé had already assembled his army, so the plan to march against him was scrapped. The Spanish general staff then considered a new objective: the recovery of Courtrai, which threatened the territory of Flanders.[11]

---

9   Hardy, *Batailles Françaises,* p.108. NB *Chevau-Légers* at the time were not the 'light horse' of later periods – they were simply battle cavalry who were less well-armoured than cuirassiers, usually wearing only buff coat and/or back and breast and a helmet. Most English Civil War horse would have been considered *Chevau-Légers* in mainland Europe. (ed.)
10   BNH, Mss. 2379, 'Sucesos', f.79.
11   Pérez, 'Relación de lo Sucedido', p 549; BNH, Mss. 2379, 1648, p.79.

5

The Path Towards the Battle

At the end of April, despite the bad weather,[1] the French army began its march east. The main body, under Condé, marched towards Péronne, where it arrived on 8 May, and where it met with Gramont and his division. The two forces coordinated their advance using different routes: Condé to the north of Arras and Gramont to the south. Condé followed Clery's route, passed Arras on 10 May, and Salis, Eterre and La Basée on 11 May. Gramont marched along the Molins road.[2] Aumale followed the route of the columns of Condé's and Gramont's troops between 8 and 13 May, and each followed parallel routes from Péronne to Ypres.[3] Condé took excessive precautions to avoid being surprised by an attack from the garrison of Lille, but nothing happened.

When they arrived at La Bassée, as the roads were muddy and flooded by heavy rains, all the French troops left using the same road leading to Armentières, where they arrived on 12 May. The French Army arrived in front of Ypres on 13 May; after a few hours detachments arrived from Dunkirk and Courtrai.[4] With the capture of Ypres, Condé's strategic objective was to secure communications between Courtrai, the entrenched camp at Dunkirk and the towns of Furnes, Bergues and Gravelines.[5]

To undertake the siege, Condé needed as many men as he could muster, so he had ordered the Compte de Palluau, *mestre de camp*, general of cavalry and Governor of Courtrai, now promoted by Condé to be lieutenant general of the army, to send him as many men as he could spare from the garrison at Courtrai to join the main army in front of Ypres, but leaving a sufficient and well-equipped garrison in the town.[6] Palluau, 'dazzled by this new

1   Wilson: *Europe's Tragedy*, p.506.
2   Marquis de Quincy, *Histoire Militaire du Regne de Louis Le Grand*, (Paris: Jean-Baptiste Delespine, 1726), p.92.
3   Aumale, *Histoire des Princes de Condé*, p.194.
4   Godley, *The Great Condé*, p.204.
5   Hardy, *Batailles Françaises*, p.101.
6   Montglat, *Collection des Mémoires*, p.96.

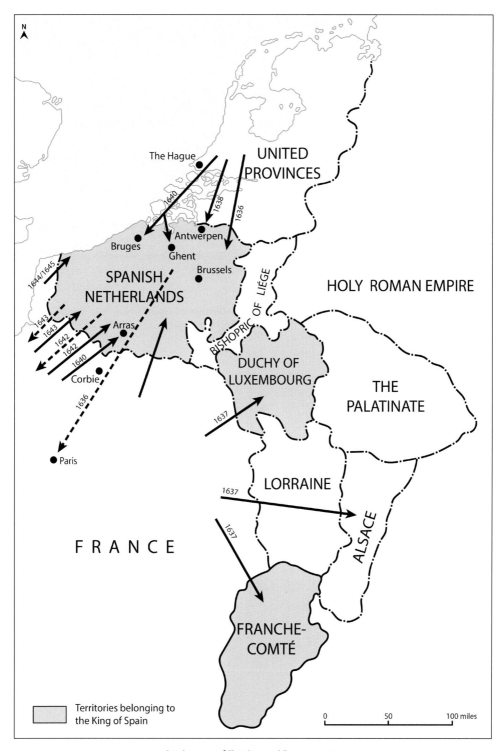

Border map of Flanders and France *c.* 1645

This map covers the main offensives in the Flanders theatre of operations (1636-1648): initially, France and the United Provinces tried to carry out simultaneous campaigns to break the defenses of Flanders; but the Cardinal-Infante stopped them and counterattacked. Spain maintained its territorial dominance until 1643, but in the campaigns of 1644-45 the French won cities on the coast of Flanders: Spain was increasingly pressed by France in all open war theatres (Flanders, Catalonia, Portugal and Italy).

rank,[7] who had 4,000 troops in the city, took half of them[8] with him and left to join the siege of Ypres, where he arrived on 12 May.[9] On the same day, *Maréchal* Josias von Rantzau arrived from Dunkirk with 3,000 men.[10] Condé thus began the siege of Ypres with an army of around 23,000 men, including Rantzau's and Palluau's forces. The French general staff was composed of the major generals who had previously served with Condé: Gramont, La Ferté-Seneterre, de Aumont de Villequier, Châtillon, Arnauld, La Moussaye and La Trémoille.[11]

The French army took up positions to completely surround Ypres. The Prince of Condé took up positions on the side of Meneene and Comines, *Maréchal* of Gramont towards Armentières; Rantzau guarded the avenues of Aire and Saint-Omer, and Palluau those of Bruges and Diksmuide.[12]

The Archduke gave no sign of marching against the French, who, surprised to have the field free, quickly took advantage of it to formalise the siege of Ypres. Condé found that the city was well garrisoned and strongly fortified, so that taking it by assault, as had initially been proposed to the French Court, was not feasible.[13] The city was defended by the Count of La Motterie, with 350 cavalry, 1,300 infantry, and a citizen militia of several thousand. The circumvallation began immediately and was completed on 19 May, when the cavalry of the Ypres garrison made a sortie, which was repulsed by the *gendarmes*, the squadron of *Chevau-Légers du Roi* and the cavalry regiment of La Meilleraye.[14] That night, the French began work on the approach trenches.

But the Spanish had not been idle; the Archduke mustered his army on 19 April and was aware of the possible actions of the French. When it became obvious that Ypres was being besieged, the Army of Flanders marched to the city's aid – in Hardy's words, 'This whole army, eager for plunder, believed itself on its way to Paris, and the rich booty there promised them more than glory.'[15]

The Army of Flanders approached the French lines around Ypres, undetected by the French, but then suddenly 'disappeared', their destination was Courtrai and they appeared in front of the city on the 18th.[16]

Antoine de Gramont, 2nd Duc de Gramont (1604–1678). Artist unknown, engraving published between 1634 and 1668 (Rijksmuseum, Amsterdam)

---

7   Montglat, *Collection des Mémoires*, p.96.
8   200 cavalry and 2,000 infantry remained as the garrison of Courtrai. Aumale, *Histoire des Princes de Condé*, p.16.
9   Montglat, *Collection des Mémoires*, p.96.
10   Aumale, *Histoire des Princes de Condé*, p.194.
11   Godley, *The Great Condé*, p.204.
12   Aumale, *Histoire des Princes de Condé*, p.194; Montglat, *Collection des Mémoires*, p.96; Quincy, *Histoire Militaire*, p.92.
13   Aumale, *Histoire des Princes de Condé*, p.195.
14   Quincy, *Histoire Militaire*, p.93.
15   Général Hardy de Perini, *Batailles Françaises, tome IV: Turenne et Condé, 1643 à 1671* (Paris: Ernest Flammarion, 1906), p .101.
16   Montglat, *Collection des Mémoires*, p.97.

Courtrai was the most advanced of all the towns that the French occupied in the territory of the River Lys, hence why the Spanish considered that this position should be eliminated as soon as possible, since it threatened Brussels, Ghent and Bruges. In February 1648 the Spaniards had tried to take the town, with a night attack on all sides, but the French garrison, after an intense two-hour battle, successfully forced them to retreat.[17] This success caused the Count of Palluau to believe that there was no longer anything to fear, and that the Spaniards, discouraged by the failure and the strength of the garrison's defence, would no longer dare to undertake anything against the town. Indeed, Palluau had stated on several occasions that the town of Courtrai was safe and could not be taken.[18]

This type of helmet, known as a morion, is associated in popular culture with the Spanish tercios, although it was used by many countries. Six small brass roses decorate the base of the helmet, on either side, but three are today missing. Possibly from The Netherlands and dated to the wide period 1600–1699. Measurements: height 23cm, length 29cm, width 23cm. (Rijksmuseum, Amsterdam. NG-NM-4495)

Courtrai's defences had been improved the previous year, and the 2,000 strong garrison, even though it was at half strength, could still present a serious defence.[19] On 19 May Condé learned that the Spanish Army was in front of Courtrai, but he believed Palluau's claims and decided to devote all his efforts to taking the city of Ypres.

As for Courtrai, the Spanish launched an attack on all the gates of the town simultaneously; the garrison was not strong enough to withstand such a great assault and retreated to the citadel, which the Spanish immediately blockaded. During the following days the Spanish bombarded the citadel and finally, after six days of siege,[20] the commander of the garrison, *Monsieur* Le Rasle, capitulated on 23 May. The speed of the capture of Courtrai showed the poor defensive capability of the French troops, as well as their defensive system; in contrast, it showed the great Spanish experience in siege operations. Thus, Courtrai, which was the most important of the French conquests in Flanders, and which held the whole of Flanders as far as Ghent in check, was lost because it was too weakly garrisoned.[21]

On 17 May, Turenne and Wrangel had defeated the Bavarians at Zusmarshausen; Mazarin was overjoyed, for at last some good military news had arrived; not only did this make his regime more secure, but it would

---

17   Montglat, *Collection des Mémoires*, p.95.
18   Montglat, *Collection des Mémoires*, p.95.
19   Maffi, *En Defensa del Imperio*, p.107.
20   BNH, Mss. 2379, 'Sucesos', f.79; Maffi, *En Defensa del Imperio*, p.107.
21   Aumale, *Histoire des Princes de Condé*, p.196. Pérez, 'Relación de lo Sucedido', p.549; Godley, *The Great Condé*, p.212; Hardy, *Batailles Françaises*, p.101; Montglat, *Collection des Mémoires*, p.96.

also make him less dependent on Condé.[22] Now he did not need to 'pamper' the young prince, to send him money and supplies as a priority, because now there was another front from which good news was coming and so he could prioritise resources to Germany; Condé would have to make do for the campaign with what he had... But the reality was not as the prime minister had imagined it would be: the operational situation of Condé's army was not very satisfactory; Condé himself wrote a report stating that his troops were underpaid, that there were more and more desertions, and that reinforcing the garrisons at Dunkirk and Ypres reduced the troops available for the campaign.

At Ypres the French launched two attacks from two different points on 20 May: *Maréchal* Arnault commanded the attack from Condé's post, and *Maréchal* Châtillon from de Gramont's camp, but both attacks were repulsed.[23]

French mounted officers of the 1640s. Detail from an engraving of the battle of Rocroi. (Riksarkivet, Stockholm)

The 21st dawned at Ypres to the thunderous roar of the guns of two French batteries firing against the city walls, and that day the French trench reached as far as the counterscarp. On the 22nd the loss of Courtrai was announced, which was a blow to the French strategy; while the siege of Ypres – which was progressing well for the French – lasted, they had only needed Courtrai to hold for at least a fortnight and then Condé could send reinforcements without jeopardising the siege of Ypres. But the news of Le Rasle's surrender was a psychological and strategic blow. Moreover, Palluau argued that it was Condé's mistake not to have left more troops in garrison, while Condé believed that Le Rasle and his men had lacked the courage to defend the city.[24] According to reports from French spies, the Archduke intended to

22   Godley, *The Great Condé*, p.207.
23   Quincy, *Histoire Militaire*, p.93.
24   Godley, *The Great Condé*, p.212; Hardy, Batailles Françaises, p.101.

march on Le Câtelet and then attack Péronne, but the imminent conclusion of the siege of Ypres caused the Archduke to change his plans.[25]

For the next few days the French filled in the moat protecting a demi-lune; the besieged, to prevent the moat from being filled, made a cavalry and infantry sortie, which was repulsed by Saint Simon's regiment.[26] On the 25th the French took the demi-lune.[27] A direct assault was attempted against the main curtain walls, but was repulsed, with the loss of *Mestre de Camp* Vieux-Pont, who commanded the *Régiment de Son Altesse Royale*.[28]

On 27 May, the French placed a mine under the curtain wall. A rumour spread through the town, and the civilian population, fearful that the town would be stormed and the civilians put to the sword with widespread pillaging, started a riot and pressured the Governor of the town to ask for terms.[29] Condé quickly agreed, eager to end the siege and regain the strategic initiative with the bulk of his army to be able to push deeper into Spanish territory.

On 29 May the surviving Spanish garrison, 350 cavalry and 1,300 infantry with 6,000 citizens who did not want to be under French rule,[30] left Courtrai and marched towards Rousselaer, where the Archduke had encamped with his army. According to French sources, the casualties in Condé's army numbered around 100 dead.[31] It was an important victory, but the loss of Courtrai weighed too heavily on everyone's memory, and the capture of Ypres did not compensate for it.

Condé proposed to the Queen that the Governor of Ypres should be Châtillon, as a reward for his list of services and his professionalism; however, Mazarin arranged for the new Governor to be Palluau, whom Condé blamed for the loss of Courtrai.[32] Many people were surprised by this choice, because the loss of Courtrai was a setback for the French campaign in Flanders and for the prestige of Condé and the French army, but Palluau was very clever in persuading Cardinal Mazarin to his side:

---

25 Quincy, *Histoire Militaire*, p.94.
26 Montglat, *Collection des Mémoires*, p.97.
27 Quincy, *Histoire Militaire*, p.93.
28 Aumale, *Histoire des Princes de Condé*, p.195; Montglat, *Collection des Mémoires*, p.96.
29 Montglat, *Collection des Mémoires*, p.97; Wilson: *Europe's Tragedy*, p.506.
30 Aumale, *Histoire des Princes de Condé*, p.195.
    Condé wrote to Mazarin lamenting that the local population helped the Spanish in the defence of their towns, while in the towns recently occupied by the French (Courtrai, Dunkirk, et cetera), France had no popular support:
    > Enemy towns are defended by the burghers and by the garrisons. In our places, the bourgeois are our mortal enemies. This winter no work has been done on any of our places on the coast, so that they can only be defended by the strength of our men; the enemy spare nothing to fortify their own, so that with 500 men they can defend a place better than we can with 1,500. Aumale, *Histoire des Princes de Condé*, p.199.
31 Hardy, *Batailles Françaises*, p.101.
32 Aumale, *Histoire des Princes de Condé*, p.197; Godley, *The Great Condé*, p.205; Montglat, *Collection des Mémoires*, p.97. Aumale comments on the anecdote that the veteran Jacques de Chastenet, Marquis de Puységur, accepted the post of *Lieutenant de Roi* at Ypres, but resigned when he learned that Palluau was to be Governor. Aumale, *Histoire des Princes de Condé*, p.198.

But as he had much wit and was very agreeable, he got the Cardinal on his side, who did not look to the services to give rewards, nor to those of the services to impose punishments.[33]

After the conquest of Ypres, Condé led his army to Béthune, where they camped. From there he asked Mazarin for instructions for planning the next campaign: the loss of Courtrai had not only resulted in the capture of its garrison, but also meant that the French army lost its forward base. *Maréchal* Josias von Rantzau's initial plan would have to be modified; Rantzau himself now proposed that the attack should be against Ostend on the coast and asked for command of the operation. Condé and Gramont considered the proposal but did not see it as feasible and therefore rejected it.[34]

Josias of Rantzau (1609–1650), engraving after the 1834 painting by Jean Alaux (1786–1864). Rantzau was a Danish military leader who served The Netherlands, Denmark, Sweden, The Holy Roman Empire, Sweden again, and finally from 1635 France. In 1635 he accompanied the Swedish chancellor Oxenstierna to France, where King Louis XIII offered him the opportunity to enter French service as colonel of a German regiment. Rantzau fought for the next years in Germany and Flanders, serving as a subordinate commander to Cardinal de La Valette, Bernhard de Saxe-Weimar, *Maréchal* de La Meilleraye, *Maréchal* de Guiche, Duc d'Anjou, and the Prince de Condé. History considers that Rantzau was braver than his military skills. He was taken prisoner by the Spanish at the Battle of Honnecourt in 1642, and by Imperial troops at the Battle of Tuttlingen in 1643. He was promoted to *maréchal de camp* on 18 February 1636, and on 22 April 1644 became *Lieutenant Général des Armées du Roi*, then on 30 June 1645 he became *Maréchal de France*. In 1649, during the Fronde, he was arrested by order of Mazarin under suspicion of treason, and imprisoned in the Bastille. He was acquitted and was released on 22 January 1650, but after his imprisonment he fell ill and died of dropsy on 4 September 1650. (Public Domain)

---

33   Montglat, *Collection des Mémoires*, p.97.
34   Godley, *The Great Condé*, p.210.

Mazarin was impressed by Rantzau's approach and, bypassing the military command structure and, in a sense, humiliating Condé – the victory at Zusmarshausen on 17 May 1648 meant he was no longer dependent on Condé to consolidate his power – he authorised Rantzau to raid Ostend on 14 June.[35]

Condé's army camped near Diksmuide, pretending to besiege it; at the same time *Maréchal* Rantzau embarked at Dunkirk with infantry, bound for Ostend. On 16 June the French attempted to land; the plan was to attack from the sea, sending the troops in boats to attack the enemy defences from the beach; but a heavy storm scattered part of the fleet away from the coast.[36] Additionally, the timing of the tides was not calculated well and thus the troops did not reach the beach properly.[37] The Spanish, led by the Marqués Sigismondo di Sfondrato, had time to react and put themselves in a state of defence: 600 men of the Piedmont regiment were killed or taken prisoner, and Rantzau himself only escaped with difficulty.[38] The operation failed, as Condé had predicted. On learning of the defeat of the expeditionary force, the Prince of Condé found himself isolated in enemy territory, so ordered his army to march towards the valley of the River Lys.[39]

Rantzau's defeat was a humiliation, and he blamed Condé because he believed that Condé had not helped him sufficiently. This caused a negative relationship between them, and Rantzau stopped answering the messages that Condé sent him. Rantzau did not inform Condé that he intended to abandon Fort Kenoque (Fort Knokke) - a fortified post located at the confluence of the Rivers Yser and Yperlée; considering that he was being cut off from his communications with the rest of the army, it was Palluau who informed Condé. For Condé, Rantzau was 'ignoring' the war and that his action of abandoning the fort could allow a Spanish force under Sfondrato to continue advancing to take Ypres. Fearing that the Spanish were starting a new large troop movement, Condé asked for reinforcements and money to improve the defences of the coast and the cities of Bergues, Furnes and Dunkirk.[40] Condé needed to have his maritime flank secured in order to be able to fight the Archduke elsewhere in Flanders, and ensuring the defence of the maritime zone would avoid being outflanked in that area.

Although it appeared that Leopold had been inactive during the first half of May, from the second his army was prepared to launch a following attack. The Spanish spies brought to the Archduke's attention that the French Army was suffering a decreasing number of troops and amount of resources, and that Paris was a nest of intrigues. Leopold had at his side a group of

---

35   Aumale, *Histoire des Princes de Condé*, p.200.

36   Montglat, *Collection des Mémoires*, p.98.

37   Godley, *The Great Condé*, p.211.

38   Maffi provides a document, written by Fuensaldaña himself, which reports that the French troops in the invasion numbered about 3,000; the defenders killed about 1,200 and captured the rest, including Rantzau himself. Maffi, *En Defensa del Imperio*, p.107.

39   Montglat, *Collection des Mémoires*, p.98.

40   Godley, *The Great Condé*, p 211. Aumale provides a letter from Condé in which, referring to Rantzau, he laments that 'I find it difficult to serve in a place where I find myself only half-heartedly obeyed...' Aumale, *Histoire des Princes de Condé*, p.201.

French exiles called The Importants. The Importants, under the leadership of Madame de Chevreuse, were plotting against the Regent and Mazarin. This intriguing woman had persuaded the Archduke that the French population was sick of its rulers and that they would welcome the arrival of the Spanish.[41]

Because of this information, the Archduke intended to invade France. After taking Courtrai, the Spaniards advanced towards Ledegem on 26 May, and arrived at Beselare on 28 May. The Spanish Army sent a strong contingent of cavalry, under the orders of the Prince de Ligne, which faced the forces under Châtillon at a large skirmish near the River Lys.[42]

The Archduke wanted to take the war to French territory, not only to move the conflict away from Flanders, but also to force the two contending armies to feed themselves at the expense the French people. On 13 June he was in Deûlémont and the next day at the Abbey of Loos, west of Lille. The main objective of incursion was to threaten the important city of Saint-Quentin; but upon realising that it was too far away, Leopold set his sights on the town of Péronne, in the Somme basin.[43] The Conde de Garcies advanced to Fonsomme, 10km northeast of Saint-Quentin, to threaten the French border cities.[44] But Spanish scouts reported that Condé's army was marching towards them, forcing Leopold to retreat east towards Landrecies and he then marched northeast, taking up positions in the area of the Mormal Forest.[45]

By mid-June, the Duc of Lorraine's cavalry, supported by strong infantry and militia from Cambrai, raided across the Somme and Oise valleys as far as Péronne, Saint-Quentin and La Fère.[46] The French border towns and

Cavalry combat, detail of an engraving by Theodorus van Kessel, 1654. (Rijksmuseum, Amsterdam)

garrisons were supposed to rise up against Louis XIV, as the group of The Importants had assured the Spanish, but nothing of the sort happened: neither the civilian population nor the troops supported the Lorrainers' raid. Vaubecourt, at the head of 800 cavalry plus 1,000 infantry of the regiment of Angien, marched through the towns of Saint-Quentin, Guise and Rocroi, provisioned the towns and drove off the looters.[47] Condé led his army on the trail of his adversary; passing Arras on 22 June, he was at Le Câtelet on 26 June. For his part, the Archduke had crossed the Scheldt, and after stopping at Catillon-sur-Sambre, he withdrew to Landrecies.

41   Aumale, *Histoire des Princes de Condé*, pp.202–207; Henri Lonchay, *La Rivalité de la France et de l'Espagne aux Pays-Bas (1635–1700)*, (Bruxelles: Hayez, 1896), pp.142–143. For more details about Madame de Chevreuse see V. Cousin, *Madame de Chevreuse* (Paris: Didier, Paris, 1862) and Georges Poisson, *La Duchesse de Chevreuse* (Paris: Librairie Académique Perrin, 1999).
42   Montglat, *Collection des Mémoires*, p.98.
43   Godley, *The Great Condé*, p.205.
44   Montglat, *Collection des Mémoires*, p.98.
45   Godley, *The Great Condé*, p.212; Hardy, *Batailles Françaises*, p.102.
46   Aumale, *Histoire des Princes de Condé*, p.208.
47   Aumale, *Histoire des Princes de Condé*, p.208.

Condé awaited instructions from Mazarin whether to attack the Spanish, forcing them into a pitched battle, to reinforce the garrisons or to focus on just one, since the Spanish could threaten all of the border towns including Guise, La Bassée or Béthune.

For the next three weeks, the French army remained around the Abbey of Vaucelles (8km north of Le Câtelet), while the Archduke remained at Maroilles (6km north-east of Landrecies); neither commander could make up his mind to attack.[48]

On 13 July, however, Condé learned that the Spaniards were marching north-west towards Lille.[49] Mazarin forbade Condé to attack them there; reports from French spies indicated that the Archduke's army outnumbered Condé's, both in numbers and artillery, and it would be a risk to engage in a battle whose loss would open the Oise valley to the Spanish, through which they could march on Paris. In the capital, the city's *Parlement* was openly hostile to the Regent, and there was a sense that a rebellion might break out.[50]

In Condé's army there were already major problems with pay and with the supply of food and some companies had mutinied. The royal treasury seemed to be empty. But the Archduke did not take advantage of a time when Condé's army was in such distress.[51]

At the time, Erlach, commander of a force of 4,000 Weimarians, was marching into France from Breisach. Following the Spanish invasion, on

Johann Ludwig von Erlach (1595–1650), unknown artist, *c.* 1650. Von Erlach was born in Bern and as a teenager entered the service of the House of Anhalt, serving as a soldier in the service of the principalities of Anhalt, Brandenburg and Braunschweig. From 1638 he served in the army of Bernhard von Weimar, when the latter was in the service of Sweden. Upon Bernard's death, Erlach became one of the four directors of the army, and on 9 October 1639 he signed the treaty by which the Duke's army passed into the service of France. From that point on Johann Ludwig von Erlach would be better known by his French name of Jean Louis d'Erlach. Erlach played an important military role, but also an important political one: during the negotiations in Münster and Osnabrück he insisted that the territories of Alsace and the Upper Rhine valley should be incorporated into the Kingdom of France in order to secure the river border. P. de Vallière, *Treue und Ehre. Geschichte der Schweizer in Fremden Diensten* (Lausanne: Deutsch von Walter Sandoz, 1940)

---

48   Aumale, *Histoire des Princes de Condé*, p.209.

49   Godley, *The Great Condé*, p.212.

50   Aumale, *Histoire des Princes de Condé*, p.209; Hardy, *Batailles Françaises,* p.102.

51   Aumale, *Histoire des Princes de Condé*, p.210. Aumale states that Condé felt despised by the Cardinal, who blamed him, as commander in chief, for the failures of this campaign – Courtrai and Furnes Aumale, *Histoire des Princes de Condé*, p.218.

20 June, Mazarin had requested that Erlach's troops march on Luxembourg and, with this diversion, relieve the threat to Picardy. On 25 June the Weimarians began their march and by 6 July were between Nancy and Château-Salins.[52]

Condé wanted to integrate these troops into his army, most especially because of the heavy casualties that he had suffered in his cavalry during the siege of Ypres and because of the Spanish guerrilla actions against French convoys and foraging parties. The official Spanish account states that during those weeks in the summer of 1648, the French had lost up to 4,000 horsemen, but this figure is probably exaggerated.[53]

Erlach was, however, an autonomous commander, used to operating with his troops on the German border. Condé was initially reluctant to propose his plan to Mazarin, for fear of antagonising him, and proposed that Erlach be stationed at Mézière, to give support in the cities of Guise or to Rocroi in case of an attack on them by the Spanish.[54]

But, pressed by the lack of resources, Condé felt it was imperative that the Weimarians join his own army: he needed to convince the Queen and Mazarin that he urgently needed reinforcements, and so on 17 July he rode from Le Câtelet to Paris to convince them. Mazarin initially disagreed with the idea that Erlach's troops should be integrated under Condé's command, and feared that this proposal would anger and make Erlach abandon French service in favour of service with the Swedes.[55] However, Condé succeeded in convincing the Queen and Mazarin.

Condé re-joined his army a few miles north of Arras on 24 July. On 27 July, the King sent a letter to Erlach ordering him to join Condé's army.[56] While waiting for Erlach to join, Condé moved his army towards the Spanish – this was not a pursuit, but a follow-up. The French Army stayed close to the Spanish, making their scouting and foraging difficult.[57] Condé moved his army to block the enemy's access to maritime Flanders and camped at a strong position at Hinges, north of Béthune, on the road to Saint-Venant.[58]

The Spanish were at Warneton, about 20 miles to the north, near Lille.[59] The Prince de Condé followed again, and the Spanish moved away from the coast, marching towards Landrecies. The Archduke's intention was to create a diversionary movement so that the French would have to withdraw from Flanders, while a force, under the Marqués Sfondrato, marched in the opposite direction to seize the coastal village of Furnes, which was defended by 1,500 men.[60] Conde Fuensaldaña was in the vanguard with a detachment

52   Aumale, *Histoire des Princes de Condé*, p.213.
53   BNH, Mss. 2379, 'Sucesos', f.79; Pérez, 'Relación de lo Sucedido', p.549; Stéphane Thion, *Les Armées Françaises de la Guerre de Trente Ans*, (Auzielle: LRT Éditions, 2008), p.163.
54   Aumale, *Histoire des Princes de Condé*, p.214.
55   Aumale, *Histoire des Princes de Condé*, p.213; Godley, *The Great Condé*, pp.213–214. Wilson affirms it was to Mazarin's credit that Erlach finally agreed to join forces with Condé. Wilson, *Europe's Tragedy*, p.506.
56   Aumale, *Histoire des Princes de Condé*, p.214.
57   Godley, *The Great Condé*, p.212.
58   Hardy, *Batailles Françaises*, p.102.
59   Godley, *The Great Condé*, p.215.
60   Montglat, *Collection des Mémoires*, p.98.

to reconnoitre the terrain for the siege trenches and the camp.[61] To secure the operation, the Archduke sent the Conde de Garcies, Governor of Cambrai, with some freshly raised troops and garrison troops, to simulate an advance towards Guise to attract Condé's attention. The Prince de Ligny remained in the interior of Flanders, at the head of understrength garrisons, with the mission of protecting the countryside.[62] The Spanish diversionary action was successful and Condé followed the Spanish Army marching towards Guise.

On 30 July, Condé received news that the Spaniards had threated Furnes (Veurne) nearby;[63] Condé approached the River Lys, taking up positions at Hinges on 2 August, ready to clear Saint-Venant, assuming that the Archduke was still with his troops at Warneton, on the Lys. Rantzau had 5,000 soldiers and the territory was crisscrossed with canals that greatly slowed the march of any detachment, so Condé believed that the defence was assured. Furthermore, Puységur left 400 soldiers in Kenoque and with 1,600 men secured the town of Hondschoote.[64]

But, for the historian Godley, the reason Condé left Furnes to its fate was that, given the proximity of Erlach's contingent, the Prince was determined to engage the Spanish in battle, and did not want to send a detachment to try to rescue a town and thus diminish his strength for a battle.[65]

The Archduke was expectant; he had forced Condé's army out of Flanders to follow them on their route to Guise, and now he had succeeded in capturing their attention so that he could take another town, Furnes, of little importance, but which could bring him further tactical success and another propaganda coup.

On one of these marches, a French scouting detachment attacked a party of Croatian irregulars in the service of Spain, capturing the officer commanding the detachment. Condé, in a cavalier attitude, released the officer, who was escorted by a trumpeter of Condé's detachment, and Condé asked the released officer to pay his respects to the Archduke. And indeed he did, the Spanish captain and a French trumpeter presented themselves at the command tent when the Archduke and General Beck were drawing up their plan of campaign. According to the French accounts:

> This prince [Archduke] responded to this honour with a stupid arrogance, and answered with such words that it would be shameful to repeat what the trumpeter reported, and Beck, to go further than the prince's discourtesy, said others more coarsely, which revealed what a low character he truly was, daring to call the Prince de Condé 'a leveret' and which Beck himself boasted he would take him to Luxembourg by the ears.[66]

61 Pérez, 'Relación de lo Sucedido', p.550.
62 BNH, Mss. 2379, 'Sucesos', f.79.
63 Aumale, *Histoire des Princes de Condé*, p.215.
64 Aumale, *Histoire des Princes de Condé*, p.215.
65 Godley, *The Great Condé*, p.215.
66 Godley, *The Great Condé*, p.205; Thion, *Les Armées Françaises*, p.164.

As the French trumpeter replied in a similar style, he was threatened with imprisonment, and finally expelled from the Spanish camp. According to this story, Condé and his officers were relaxing in the command tent when La Moussaye entered with the Brussels' *Gazette*, in which the enemy, furious at the loss of Ypres but exultant at the capture of Courtrai, reported the Archduke's words that he was, 'looking everywhere for the army of the Prince of Condé and that he would give wine to whoever found this army and brought him news of it.'[67] Condé took this in good humour, mocking the Archduke's high-handed attitude, but when the embassy, returning from the Spanish camp, entered and explained the contents of the Archduke's and Beck's statements, Condé was incensed and vowed that he would spare the Archduke the trouble of searching for him, if the latter dared to come out of the forest where he had entrenched his army.[68]

A variant of this story explains that the Archduke used propaganda to undermine French morale after he took Furnes.[69] Expressly forgetting the loss of Ypres, Leopold taunted the French that he had searched for them in the region, but had not found them because they had fled from him. This news appeared in the Brussels and Antwerp *Gazette*, and when the news reached the ears of Condé's army officers, they were exceedingly angry. Condé did not lose his temper: he gathered his officers together and reassured them that they would soon be found and the world would see who feared whom.[70]

Spanish artillery and assault columns of musketeers. Detail of an engraving of the siege of La Bassée in 1642. Petrus Rucholle, 1642. (Rijksmuseum, Amsterdam)

---

67 Aumale, *Histoire des Princes de Condé*, p.219; Godley, *The Great Condé*, p.205; Thion, *Les Armées Françaises*, p.164.
68 Godley, *The Great Condé*, p.205; Thion, *Les Armées Françaises*, p.164.
69 For Wilson, the military success of the conquest of Furnes was small, but the prestige of the action for the Spanish meant a triple failure for the French: the loss of a town and the loss of prestige at home and abroad, in the negotiations that were taking place in Osnabrück and Münster. Wilson, *Europe's Tragedy*, p.506.
70 Godley, *The Great Condé*, p.216.

At Furnes, the Spanish Army dug siege trenches on 29 July and quickly set up batteries to bombard the town. As a result, the Spanish reached the counterscarp on 31 July, and the following night, having crossed the moat, they launched an assault. The Governor of Furnes, *Monsieur* Le Boquet, seeing that the situation was untenable, surrendered on 2 August, and the next day they were escorted to Dunkirk.[71] Two days later, the Spanish Army marched towards the Lys.[72] Condé had the concern and diplomacy to write to Mazarin to exonerate Le Boquet of any blame, as the garrison was totally isolated and without any hope of a relief force.[73]

The French Army was still encamped at Hinges, from where it controlled the towns of Estaires and Saint-Venant; the town of Saint-Venant and the castle of Estaires were the only fortified posts that the French had retained on the Lys.[74]

Fuensaldaña returned to the Warneton camp with the victorious troops from Furnes. On 11 August, the Archduke left Loos, while Fuensaldaña left Warneton, the two columns converging at Armentières, where they united and followed the course of the River Lys, upstream to take the small fortress of Estaires, on the banks of the River Lys, 18km north-east of Béthune.[75] Spanish spies informed the Archduke of the French Army's position, and the Archduke thought he could reach the town before any possible French reinforcements; so, at dusk that day, the Spanish Army began the march, which lasted all night. By the morning of the 12th, the Archduke was in front of the castle, the guns were positioned and the fortress, which was defended by a garrison of 40 to 50 French soldiers, began to be fired upon. That same evening the French surrendered.[76]

At the sound of cannon fire on 12 August, the French army began the relief march from the camp at Hinges; Condé put half of his troops into line of battle in front of the enemy and sent Gramont to Merville (5km west), and then towards Neufberquin. Condé went with another detachment with the aim of saving Estaires.[77] However, the roads were blocked and defended by strong Spanish detachments; the French attacked and although they managed to take some, the Archduke sent reinforcements and the French could make no further progress. Condé's army concentrated at Merville to resume the march; meanwhile, the Spanish guns continued firing, but at dusk they fell silent: the town had surrendered.[78] The French vanguard stayed at Merville, west of Estaires, from where it left the next day to re-join the rest of the army, which had remained under Gramont's command.[79]

---

71   Aumale, *Histoire des Princes de Condé*, p.216.

72   Montglat, *Collection des Mémoires*, p.99.

73   Godley, *The Great Condé*, p.215; Hardy, *Batailles Françaises*, p.102.

74   Aumale, *Histoire des Princes de Condé*, p.219

75   Aumale, *Histoire des Princes de Condé*, pp.194 & 220.

76   Aumale, *Histoire des Princes de Condé*, p.220; Pérez, 'Relación de lo Sucedido', p.550.

77   Aumale, *Histoire des Princes de Condé*, p.220.

78   Aumale, *Histoire des Princes de Condé*, p.194, Godley, *The Great Condé*, p.216; Hardy, Batailles Françaises, p.102; BNH, Mss. 2379, 'Sucesos', f.79; Montglat, Collection des Mémoires, p.98; Pérez, 'Relación de lo Sucedido', p.550.

79   Hardy, Batailles Françaises, p.102.

Condé found that they were losing the strategic initiative and could only pursue the Spaniards, but never catch or overtake them. This led him to lament that his army was underprepared, undersupplied and under reinforced; mutinies had broken out in some places and in some companies, due to lack of food and of pay.[80] All available resources were being sent to Germany; Condé bought 1,000 muskets out of his own pocket: half were sent to Palluau at Ypres and half to Mazarin's dragoon regiment.[81]

FRANCOIS DE L'HOS-   PITAL DV HALLIER
Comte de Rosnay Chlier des   *ordres du Roy, Mar.ᵃᵉ de Fran.*
Capᵗᵉ lieut.ᵗ de la compᵗᵉ des   *deux cens hommes d'armes*
de sa Maᵗᵉˢ seul lieut. gnâl es   *Prouᵗᵉ de Champᵗᵉ et Brie.*

François de l'Hôpital du Hallier (1583–1660), engraving by Michel Lasne (c. 1590–1667). The exact date of this work is unknown, but from the appearance of l'Hôpital, it would be close to that of the battle of Rocroi in 1643, when the general was 60 years old. L'Hôpital is in a cuirass, and displays the typical French fashion in hair and facial hair. The veteran general, who began his military career at a young age, rose to the rank of *Maréchal* de France. (National Gallery of Art, Washington, D.C.)

Condé needed Erlach's troops to join his army as soon as possible, and he would then seek battle against Leopold. In the meantime, neither of the two generals, Condé and Leopold, intended to engage in battle. However, skirmishing occurred: the Spanish secured several bridges over the Lawe and appeared at La Gorgue and Lestrem. Condé led a detachment to drive the Spanish out of La Gorgue and a detachment, the regiments of Persan, the Guards and Arnault's *Carabiniers* commanded by Châtillon, defeated the cavalry of Conde de Bucquoy at Lestrem.[82]

The Archduke decided that he should press harder and relieve the pressure of an invasion of Flanders, thus the Spanish Army set out for La Bassée and Lens.

On 14 August, Erlach's troops arrived in Arras. Condé sent *Maréchal* Vaubecour from Béthune, with a small detachment towards Souchez, to confront Erlach. On the morning of 16 August Erlach arrived at Béthune, with 3,500 veteran troops.[83] Condé had imagined that this army was larger and he now had 16,000 men with 18 guns, while the Spanish numbered about 18,000 men and 38 guns.[84] Condé had had to detach 6 battalions of French infantry to reinforce the Rantzau contingent; and in addition, he had sent 4 battalions to reinforce the garrisons on the border between Guise and Rocroi.[85]

During the morning of 17 August, a Spanish force of about 1,200 cavalry approached the area to observe the French advance and ascertain their strength.[86]

80   Aumale, *Histoire des Princes de Condé*, p.209.
81   Godley, *The Great Condé*, p.213.
82   Aumale, *Histoire des Princes de Condé*, p.222; Godley, *The Great Condé*, p.216.
83   Aumale, *Histoire des Princes de Condé*, p.223. Hardy and Montglat state that there were about 4,000 troops (Hardy, Batailles Françaises, p.102; Montglat, *Collection des Mémoires*, p.99). Aumale notes that 'Erlach had left many people behind, nearly all his Englishmen. The abuse of green fruit and Moselle wine had considerably reduced his forces. Aumale, *Histoire des Princes de Condé*, p.224.
84   Wilson: *Europe's Tragedy*, p.506.
85   Godley, *The Great Condé*, p.217.
86   Thion, *Les Armées Françaises*, p.164.

Condé's first offensive move, after being reinforced by Erlach, was to retake Estaires: to accomplish this he sent *Monsieur* Villequier, who recaptured the town on 18 August by an aggressive assault, capturing its garrison of 300 men.[87] Not only was a strategic position recaptured, but this also boosted the morale of the army, since after the capture of Ypres at the beginning of the campaign, it had all been bad news for the French.

On 16 August, Gramont informed Condé that the Spanish observation positions on the right bank of the Lawe were empty. There was no sign of whether the Archduke's army was marching towards La Bassée or returning to attack maritime Flanders. Condé ordered Villequier to make sure that the enemy had not recrossed the Lys; in the meantime, Condé himself led a detachment to reconnoitre south-east.[88]

Also on 16 August, the Spanish Army began the march towards Lens, following the north bank of the Neuf-Fossé (La Bassée Canal) and crossed the River Deule at Don.[89] The next day, they recrossed the Deule at Pont-à-Vendin,[90] and that night, the Governor of La Bassée, *Monsieur* Le Plessis-Bellière, wrote to Condé that the Spanish had passed through Pont-à-Vendin and were on the way to Lens. Condé received the message from La Bassée early on 18 August, in the field in front of Estaires, after having taken it. Condé, with a small escort, went ahead of his army to reconnoitre the area while Gramont led the army, heading towards La Bassée. Condé was looking for a battle, he believed that with Erlach's reinforcements he could successfully engage with the Spanish and so great was his eagerness to fight, that he feared Leopold was still moving southward and he would not be able to catch him.[91]

According to Aumale however, Condé was afraid that the Spaniards would escape him: and that they could attack the places on the Oise and the Meuse. Therefore, he ordered Vidame to march with four infantry regiments, from Arras to the area of Guise and Rocroi, since the Spaniards could attack Bergues and the other coastal towns, from their positions in Furnes and Saint-Omer. Meanwhile Vaubecourt's force – with the regiments of Angien, Noirmoutier, du Roi, Gamaches, two companies of *gendarmes*, and some Guards Écossaise – was to march towards the coast and to garrison Dunkirk.[92]

On 18 August the Spanish appeared in front of Lens, having the river on their side as flank protection. Lens was a small town in the county of Artois. It is perched on a hill 18km north of Arras and 17km south of La Bassée. A small river (the Souchez) flows at the foot of the hill on the Arras side. The landscape on the La Bassée side is made up of two large undulating plains, whose hills and valleys descend imperceptibly. This place has been taken and retaken several times, by both contenders; in the words of Isaac de La

87   Aumale, *Histoire des Princes de Condé*, p.225; Montglat, *Collection des Mémoires*, p.99; Quincy, *Histoire Militaire*, p.94.
88   Aumale, *Histoire des Princes de Condé*, p.224.
89   Aumale, *Histoire des Princes de Condé*, p.194.
90   Godley, *The Great Condé*, p.217.
91   Godley, *The Great Condé*, p.217.
92   Aumale, *Histoire des Princes de Condé*, p.225.

THE BATTLE OF LENS 1648

Operations of the 1648 campaign

The French offensive of 1648 aimed to conquer the important place of Ypres. Condé established his headquarters at Arras (1) and marched towards Ypres, where he was joined by troops from Dunkirk and Courtrai (2). While the French besieged Ypres, the Spanish advanced from Brussels (A) and conquered the city of Courtrai, which had a diminished garrison (B).

Condé moved his army towards Béthune (3); An amphibious raid against Ostend was also attempted, but it failed with many losses (4). The Spanish tried to divert the attention of the French, carrying out continuous marches, from Courtrai to Lille (C), from Lille to Landrecies (D) and from Landrecies to Warneton (E); the French army followed them (5-7). The Spanish objective was to conquer Furnes (F) and after achieving it, their next objective was Lens (G). The French lagged behind the Spanish (8-9).

Peyrère, Condé's aide-de-camp, 'he who was master of the countryside, was master of Lens.'[93] Hardy said, 'Leopold's generals excelled in the choice and organisation of the defensive positions at Lens.'[94]

The Spanish Army camped on the top of Rideau hill, where they placed their artillery in two lines, and fortified their camp.[95] However, the French, in the early hours of 18 August, still did not know exactly where the Spanish were:

> They were in Don, some said; others reported their presence at Pont-à-Vendin; there was enough to puzzle over. Is the Spaniard heading east or south? Do they want to gain the Oise valley? Perhaps penetrate into Champagne? or go down the Somme by overturning our positions at Artois?[96]

When Condé heard that the siege of Lens had begun, as the cannonading could be heard from the French camp, he rejoiced that the enemy had been located. The Archduke had learned of the arrival of the Weimarians, and that the two armies were now fairly evenly matched in numbers: he now knew that sooner or later there would be a battle, so his aim was to find a strategic position and suitable ground to fight the battle.[97]

Condé, with a small escort, passed through La Bassée, and from there he could see the Spanish Army in the distance, near Lens.[98] He continued his scouting and by mid-afternoon returned to La Bassée, where Gramont and the army had arrived. He assembled his staff and arranged the order of battle for the next day, when he would offer battle.[99] That same evening, Lens surrendered.[100] The town itself had lost the splendour it had once had, because its walls had been greatly weakened, the town having been taken by both sides on several occasions. However, Lens was at the centre of a plain and of a crossroads, controlling the routes to Béthune, La Bassée, Arras and Douai.[101]

On the morning of 19 August, the French Army began the march from La Bassée; it consisted of 45 cavalry squadrons and 12 infantry battalions. However, the numbers were far from magnificent: of the 29 regiments (22 French and 7 foreign), which were initially assigned to the campaign, 11 of them were divided up in various towns as garrisons and were only partly available for the Battle of Lens; additionally, they initially had a theoretical strength of 1,500 men, but after several months, some of them could now count on little more than 300 effectives.[102] And as for pay, as *Parlement* was at odds with the Queen and Mazarin, it had not agreed to increase

---

93   Hardy, *Batailles Françaises*, p.102.
94   Hardy, *Batailles Françaises*, p.103.
95   Thion, *Les Armées Françaises*, p.164.
96   Aumale, *Histoire des Princes de Condé*, p.226.
97   Aumale, *Histoire des Princes de Condé*, p.217.
98   Aumale, *Histoire des Princes de Condé*, p.227; Godley, *The Great Condé*, p.217.
99   Godley, *The Great Condé*, p.217.
100 Aumale, *Histoire des Princes de Condé*, p.194.
101 Aumale, *Histoire des Princes de Condé*, p.233.
102 Thion, *Les Armées Françaises*, p.132.

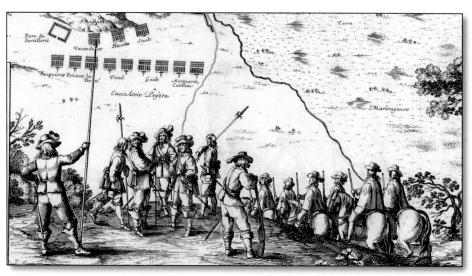

French cavalry and infantry during the siege of Rosas in 1645. Sébastien de Pontault, Sieur de Beaulieu, *Les Glorieuses Victoires de Louis le Grand* (Paris; Chez l'Autheur, 1694). (Riksarkivet, Stockholm)

contributions to pay the army – the available funds had been earmarked for troops in Germany – so Condé's troops had, over the course of the last 8 months, received only half pay.[103]

Condé moved his army towards the city in the classic three-body deployment. Figures provided by various historians indicate that the French force consisted of about 6,000 cavalry and 16,000 to 18,000 infantry.[104]

The right flank, commanded by Condé himself, was composed of 17 cavalry squadrons, in two lines: the first, under *Lieutenant Général* Aumont-Villequier, assisted by *Maréchals de Camp* Arnauld and La Moussaye Villequier, with 9 squadrons (*Gardes de Monsieur* le Prince de Condé, Chappes, Coudray-Montpensier, Salbrick, Vidame d'Amiens, Ravenel and Le Vilette – formerly Gassion); the second line, with Claude de la Trémoille, Marquis de Noirmoutiers as commander, made up of 8 squadrons (*Son Altesse d'Orléans*, La Meilleraye, Streef, Saint Simon, Bussy-Almory, Beaujeu).[105]

---

103 Hardy, Batailles Françaises, p.104.

104 M. Desormeaux. *Histoire de Louis de Borbon, Second du Nom, Prince de Condé*, tome 1 (Paris: chez Saillant, 1766), p.58; Godley, *The Great Condé*, p.218; Hardy, Batailles Françaises, p.104; Quincy, *Histoire Militaire*, p.95; Thion, *Les Armées Françaises*, p.132.

105 Desormeaux. *Histoire de Louis de Borbon*, tome 1, p.218; Hardy, *Batailles Françaises*, p.104; Quincy, *Histoire Militaire*, p.95; Thion, *Les Armées Françaises*, p.132; Gramont describes the composition of the French right wing somewhat differently:

This was the disposition of the army: the Prince de Condé took the right wing of the cavalry, which consisted of nine squadrons: one of his guards, two of *Son Altesse Royale*, one of the *Grand-Maistre*, one of Saint Simon, one of Bussy, one of Streiff, one of Harcourt le Vieux and one of Beaujeu; Villequier was *lieutenant général* under him; Field *Maréchals de Camp* Noirmoutier and La Moussaye; the Marquis de Fors was the *Maréchal de Camp* and Beaujeu was commander of the cavalry of that brigade.

The second cavalry line, commanded by *Maréchal de Camp* Arnault, was composed of eight squadrons: one from Arnault, two from Chappes, one from Coudray, one from Salbrich, one from Vidame and two from Villette (Thion, *Les Armées Françaises*, p.160).

Aumale also gives a different composition:

First line: *Gardes de Monsieur le Prince, Son Altesse Royale* (2 squadrons), *Grand-Maistre*, Saint Simon, Bussy, Stref, Harcourt le Vieil, Deaujeu.

Gaspard de Coligny, Duc de Châtillon,[106] commanded the centre, which contained all of the infantry, in two lines: [107] in the first line, 7 infantry battalions (*Gardes Françaises*, *Gardes Suisses*, *Gardes Écossaises*, Persan, Picardy, *Son Altesse Royale d'Orléans* and Erlach); the second line, with 5 infantry battalions (Conti, Condé, La Reine, Razilly and Mazarin *Italien*),[108] and in the space between the two infantry lines were 6 squadrons of *gendarmes*[109] (companies of Condé, Schomberg, La Reine, Duc d'Orléans, d'Enghien, Conti, Longueville and Marcillac).[110] Châtillon's subordinates

Antoine III de Gramont, *Maréchal* de France (1604–1678), by an unknown engraver, *c.* 1670. The portrait shows the *Maréchal* during his retirement, when he spent long periods in his lands in Bayonne or in Bidache; in the latter castle he built an extensive library. (Public Domain)

Second line: Chappes (2 squadrons), Ravenel, Coudray, Salbric, Vidame, Villette (2 squadrons) (Aumale, *Histoire des Princes de Condé*, p.228).

Guthrie also presents a different detail of the composition of the French flank:

First line, with 9 squadrons: *Gardes de Monsieur le Prince de Condé*, *Gardes de Son Altesse de Orléans* (2 squadrons), La Meilleraye, Saint Simon, Bussy, Streif, Harcourt, Beaujeu.

Second line, with 8 squadrons: Chappes (2 squadrons), Ravenel, Coudray, Salbrick, Vidame, Villiette (2 squadrons). (William P. Guthrie, *Batallas de la Guerra de los Treinta Años. Segundo Período* (Madrid: Ediciones Salamina, 2017, p.295).

106 Aumale, despite his fervour for Condé, introduces the following question, casting doubt on Condé's slight recklessness:

Is Châtillon to be left alone in the centre with two *Maréchals de Camp* to command 12 battalions and the *gendarmerie*, which might be said to be the main body of this army? No doubt a single impulse is needed there; the chiefs of the infantry and the *gendarmerie* are very expert agents of execution; but if Châtillon is killed or wounded, if he is captured, who will replace him? (Aumale, *Histoire des Princes de Condé*, p.231).

107 Here again we have Guthrie detailing another composition:

First line, 7 battalions: *Gardes Françaises* (2 battalions), *Gardes Ecossaises*, *Gardes Suisses*, *Picardie-Orléans*, Erlach, Perrault, Persan.

Second line, 5 battalions: Conti, Condé, La Reine, Erlach-Razilly and Mazarin, formed by Italians).

Between the two lines of infantry were 6 squadrons, with a total of 12 companies, of cavalry: *La Reine*, Condé, Longueville, Conti, gendarmes Duc d'Orléans, *Chevau Léger* d'Orléans and d'Enghien (Guthrie, *Batallas de la Guerra de los Treinta Años*, p.295).

108 According to Hardy and Aumale, the garrison from La Bassé and the *régiment* Rokeby formed the 1st battalion (Aumale, *Histoire des Princes de Condé*, p.228; Guthrie, *Batallas de la Guerra de los Treinta Años*, p.296; Hardy, *Batailles Françaises*, p.104). Gramont specifies that together with the battalion of *La Reine* they formed 300 men of the garrison of La Bassée; the battalion of Dazilly he calls 'Rasilly' (Thion, *Les Armées Françaises*, p.160).

109 *Gendarmes et Chevau-Légers d'Ordonnance: Compagnies du Roi, de la Reine*, de Condé, de Longueville, de Conti, *Chevau-Légers* d'Orléans et d'Enghien: in total, 12 companies in 6 squadrons (Aumale, *Histoire des Princes de Condé*, p.228).

110 Godley, *The Great Condé*, p.218; Hardy, *Batailles Françaises*, p.104–105; Thion, *Les Armées Françaises*, p.132.

Gaspard de Coligny, Duc de Châtillon (1584–1646). Portrait by Willem Jacobsz. Delff, 1631 (Rijksmuseum, Amsterdam)

were *Monsieurs* Villemesle and Beauregard.[111] *Maréchal* de Gramont commanded the left wing, with *Monsieu*r de Lainville as his second in command, with 16 squadrons formed in two lines:[112] 9 in the first line (2 squadrons from Les Bains, 2 squadrons from La Ferté-Senneterre, 2 squadrons from Gramont, Mazarin, Arnault's *carabiniers*, the *Gardes* from Gramont and the *Gardes* from La Ferté-Senneterre – the latter two in a combined squadron), under the command of *Lieutenant Général* La Ferté-Seneterre, seconded by *Maréchal de Camp* Saint-Mégrin; the second line, the other 7 squadrons are under the command of *Maréchal de Camp* Du Plessis-Bellière (Chemerault, Meille, Lillebonne, Gesvres).[113]

At the head of the infantry, 18 guns were commanded by Timoléon de Cossé-Brissac, *Lieutenant du Grand-Maître*, and the two artillery commissioners, Des Hayes and La Guette.[114]

In the rear was Erlach, with the rank of *lieutenant général* and Rasilly as *Maréchal de*

---

111 Thion, *Les Armées Françaises*, p.160.
112 Aumale provides another composition of this wing's squadrons:
 First line: *Gardes du Maréchal de Gramont et de La Ferté* (4 esquadrons), *Carabins*, Mazarin, (2 squadrons), Gramont (2 squadrons), La Ferté-Senneterre (2 squadrons), Beins (2 squadrons).
 Second line: Roquelaure, Gesvres, Lillebonne, Noirlieu (2 squadrons), Meille, Chemerault (Aumale, *Histoire des Princes de Condé*, p.228).
 Guthrie provides a slightly different composition:
 First line, 9 squadrons: Gardes du *Maréchal* de Gramont and de La Ferté, *Carabiniers*, Mazarin (2 squadrons), Gramont (2 squadrons), La Ferté-Senneterre (2 squadrons), Venis (2 squadrons).
 Second line, 7 squadrons: Roquelaure, Gesvre, Lillebonne, Noitlieu (2 squadrons), Meille, Chemerault (Guthrie, *Batallas de la Guerra de los Treinta Años*, p.295).
113 Godley, *The Great Condé*, p.218; Hardy, *Batailles Françaises*, p.105; Quincy, *Histoire Militaire*, p.96. Gramont adds that 'La Ferté was lieutenant-general; Saint Maigrin was field marshal; Linville was battle marshal and the Comte de Lillebonne was the cavalry commander of this brigade'. Again, Gramont provides different information regarding the second line of the left wing; it was composed of seven squadrons: one from Roquelaure, one from Gesvres, one from Lillebonne, two from Noirlieu, one from Meille and one from Chemerault (Thion, *Les Armées Françaises*, p.160). Aumale details a different composition in the second line:
 Second line: Roquelaure, Gesvres, Lillebonne, Noirlieu (2 squadrons), Meille, Chemerault
 (Aumale, *Histoire des Princes de Condé*, p.228).
114 Aumale, *Histoire des Princes de Condé*, p.228; Godley, *The Great Condé*, p.218; Hardy, *Batailles Françaises*, p.105; Quincy, *Histoire Militaire*, p.96.

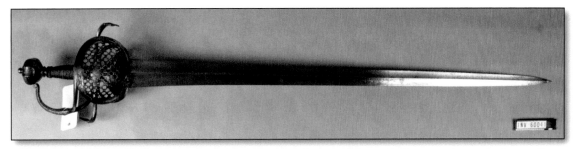

Cavalry sword, with a total length of 1,120mm, length of the blade of 910mm, with a width of 53mm, and a weight of 1,250g. The blade is double edged, at the hilt it is quite wide, but it tapers towards the tip. On both sides it is adorned at the hilt with engraved ornamentation and on the one side with an image of Bernard de Saxe-Weimar in a medallion frame. On the other side, in addition to the ornamentation, there is a portrait of Gustav II Adolph within the same type of frame as that of Saxe-Weimar. However, on the blade it has the inscription *ME FECIT SOLINGEN* 1652 (I was manufactured in Solingen in 1652). All this suggests that the hilt and guard of the sword were manufactured around 1630 and that they belonged to an officer of the regiments of Bernard of Saxe-Weimar, when he was in the service of Sweden. The blade was later replaced in 1652. (Armémuseum, AM.060041)

Camp,[115] with 6 squadrons of his Weimarian troops (Fabry, 3 squadrons of Erlach, Sirot, Ruvigny).[116]

It is difficult to establish any uniform composition of units at this time; Guthrie says that the French battalions should have numbered around 600–700, deployed 8 ranks deep, and the cavalry companies 150–200 men, 4–5 ranks deep.[117]

Condé, as was his custom, led the vanguard on the march, while the French army on the march moved across the plain of Lens. The French passed through Loos and soon discovered the enemy established on the southern edge of the plain.[118]

Condé halted his army, to redress the lines, and awaited any movement from the enemy army. He galloped to the front line and saluted the senior officers; the infantry cheered him waving their hats, the cavalry drew their swords. When the deployment was completed between Loos and Mazingarbe, the French discovered the enemy squadrons in the vicinity of Lens;[119] but they could see only the cavalry squadrons: from the visible insignia, the French estimated that there were about 40 squadrons in front of them.

---

115 Thion, *Les Armées Françaises*, p.160.
116 Godley, *The Great Condé*, p.218; Thion, *Les Armées Françaises*, p.132. Aumale and Guthrie agree: Erlach (2 squadrons), Sirot (2 squadrons) and Ruvigny (2 squadrons) (Aumale, *Histoire des Princes de Condé*, p.228; Guthrie, *Batallas de la Guerra de los Treinta Años*, p.295).
117 Guthrie, *Batallas de la Guerra de los Treinta Años*, p.296.
118 Aumale, *Histoire des Princes de Condé*, p.232.
119 According to Aumale, the distance that separated them was about 2.5km (Aumale, *Histoire des Princes de Condé*, p.233).

6

The Battle

Faced with a decisive battle, Condé took every precaution, and issued three very important orders for the whole army:

> Each regiment or squadron was to observe how the units on either side were doing, to keep them all in line;
> The units were to advance at a slow pace, especially at the moment of attack;
> The enemy was to be allowed to fire first.[1]

Monsieur de Fors, *maréchal de battaille*, watched the lines, supervising the alignments, while calling out Condé's orders to the troops as they deployed.[2]

For Aumale:

> The distances between the lines, the intervals between tactical units are precisely regulated to facilitate the march, the line passes in advance or retreat, and all the evolutions that combat may require.[3]

Condé wanted his troops to maintain discipline at all times: if units advanced at a slow pace, it was easier for officers to maintain order, and the faster they went, the more fatigue they risked upon arriving at the attack on the enemy line. As for letting the Spaniards fire first, this was a risky option, since a volley could cause heavy casualties, but it was also true that the reloading process of seventeenth to nineteenth century muskets was slow, so that a unit that had fired would take around 30 seconds to be fully reloaded. In addition, a premature salvo could be ineffective, as the accuracy of muskets was low. Therefore, the order to fire second would surely guarantee a more devastating effect on the enemy line.[4]

---

1   Godley, *The Great Condé*, p.218; Thion, *Les Armées Françaises*, p.160.
2   Aumale, *Histoire des Princes de Condé*, p.232; Desormeaux. *Histoire de Louis de Borbon*, tome 1, p.75; Hardy, *Batailles Françaises*, p.106; Charles Malo, *Champs de Bataille de France* (Paris: Hachette, 1899), p.72; BNH, Mss. 2379, 'Sucesos', f.198; Quincy, *Histoire Militaire*, p.96.
3   Aumale, *Histoire des Princes de Condé*, p.232.
4   Godley, *The Great Condé*, p.218; Quincy, *Histoire Militaire*, p.96.

The Spanish Army numbered about 18,000 soldiers in 62 squadrons and 12 battalions.[5] The French were marching from the vicinity of the village of Loos, while the Spanish had placed their line between Lens and Liévin, anchored on the stream of La Souchez. During the night, the Spanish camp, established at Liévin, was better fortified, with parapets and ditches.[6] The Spanish line of battle ran parallel to the line linking Lens to the village of Liévin, on a gentle rise.[7]

There is no exhaustive account of the units that took part in the battle in the Spanish sources; however, the French sources indicate, in their lists of prisoners, to which units they belonged, so that the Spanish order of battle can be partially reconstructed.[8]

The Spanish left flank was on a hill in front of which there was a series of ravines.[9] The first line of cavalry, under the Prince de Salm, on this flank consisted of 10 squadrons of the Walloon regiments of Luneville, Prince Louis of Savoy, Garnier, Toledo and Bastin (other accounts mention the regiments of Daygree and Auton in addition). In the second line, under Lignéville, there were also 10 squadrons, from the units of the Lorrainer regiments of Montauban, Ligniville, Châtelet, Hacquefort, Fauge, Mondragon and Montmorency (the regiments of Melin and Valentin are mentioned in other accounts).

At the centre of the Spanish deployment, the Archduke had placed his command position. The front line consisted of 16 infantry battalions, under Beck, which were protected by thickets, which gave them good natural cover to hinder the French advance:[10] the Spanish tercios of Solis, Bonifaz and Desa; the German tercios of Monroy and Beck, the Walloon tercios of Lannoy, La Motterie and Grosbandon; the Spanish tercio of Vargas; the Italian tercios of Bentivoglio and Guasco; the Lorrainer regiments of Touvenin, Silly and Clinchcamp; and the Irish tercios of de Marais, Sinot and Plunkett; and the Lorrainer regiments of de Remion and L'Huilier. The number of units exceeds 12 battalions, so that in each battalion there would have been companies from different

Portrait by Paulus Pontius, of Jean de Beck (1588–1648), between 1616 and 1657. (Rijksmuseum, Amsterdam)

---

5   Aumale, *Histoire des Princes de Condé*, p.236; Hardy, *Batailles Françaises*, p.112; Thion, *Les Armées Françaises*, p.160

6   Hardy, *Batailles Françaises*, p.103.

7   Godley, *The Great Condé*, p.219.

8   Aumale, *Histoire des Princes de Condé*, p.233.

9   Thion, *Les Armées Françaises*, p.160.

10   Thion, *Les Armées Françaises*, p.160.

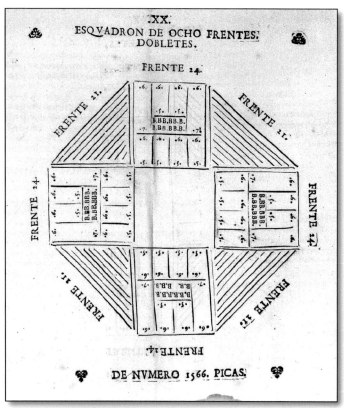

:XX.
ESQVADRON DE OCHO FRENTES.
DOBLETES.

FRENTE 24.

FRENTE 21.

FRENTE 24.

FRENTE 24.

FRENTE 21.

DE NVMERO 1566. PICAS.

Illustration from *Sargento Mayor* Miguel Lorente Bravo, *Compendio Militar y Tratado de Escuadrones* (Madrid: 1643). Throughout the seventeenth century, numerous books written by former officers were written and published in Spain. In these battle tactics, unit organisation and the logistics of armies were explained. All of the books also taught how to *escuadronear*, that is, form ad hoc units based on the available troops, the terrain and the enemy. Using complex mathematical formulas, it was the task of the *sargento mayor* of the tercio to be able to place the companies in this type of unit. In this illustration, as complex as it is implausible, a total of 1,566 pikemen are available and a 360° self-defence unit is shown: 4 rectangular squadrons are formed, with 24 front and 11 deep soldiers, as well as 4 triangular squadrons, of 21 man frontage and 11 ranks deep, which are inserted in the formation.

CAROLVS ALBERTVS DE LONGVEVAL COMES DE BVQVOY ET DE GRATZEN, BARO DE VAVX ET DE ROSEN BERGHE COMIT: HANNONIÆ. GVBERNATOR.&

Charles Albert de Longueval, Conde de Bucquoy (1607–1663). Artist unknown, engraving published between 1637 and 1668. (Rijksmuseum, Amsterdam)

tercios and regiments, which was not an uncommon practice in the Spanish infantry.

The sources are contradictory regarding the location of the cavalry that supported the infantry; in some sources, the Conde de Fuensaldaña, who had 15 squadrons under his command and which would act as a reserve, was behind the infantry. However, according to Aumale, the cavalry was interspersed among the infantry; in the front line were cuirassier cavalry detachments: 4 small squadrons of Michael (Walloon); 3 small squadrons of Diego (Walloon); 4 squadrons of Salm's regiment (Lorrainer); 3 small squadrons of Saint-Amour (Walloon).[11] The Croats could have been placed in the first line of infantry or on the flanks of the deployment. There would also have been a second line, although only consisting of 2 squadrons of cuirassiers of the Archduke's and of Fuensaldaña's guards.

Finally, a third line, consisting of the remaining 6 infantry battalions: Verduisant and Gondrecourt regiments (Lorrainer); Wanghen and Arias regiments (German); Hous and Chastelain regiments (German and Lorrainer); Berlau and Anselm regiments (German

---

11   Aumale, *Histoire des Princes de Condé*, p.235.

and English); Tercio de Toledo (Spanish); Tercios of Bruay and Crèvecoeur (Walloon).[12]

The Spanish right wing, the Flanders cavalry, consisting of 27[13] squadrons of Flemish cuirassiers, formed in two lines, under the command of Conde de Bucquoy, located under the ramparts of Lens, in the present suburb of Saint Laurent, towards Notre-Dame de Bon-Secours. In the first line, 12 squadrons, consisting of the Bucquoy (Germans), Savary (Germans), Prince de Ligne (Walloons), Brouck (Germans) regiments and the Walloon companies of Ris and Meinssague. In the second line, under the command of the Prince de Ligne, 12 Walloon squadrons, from the companies of Sandoy, Scandalberg, Erland, Gonni, Hurc and Scalar.

The Comte de Saint-Amour, general of artillery, placed his 38 guns on the ridges, to bombard the plain of Lens from a distance. The terrain of the battlefield was essentially flat – ideal for cavalry manoeuvres.[14]

A common feature of the Spanish units, was that at the time their battalions consisted of about 500–600 men, like the Imperial battalions, although after an intense campaign, this number could be reduced to less than 500, and would be deployed in ranks of up to 10 men deep. The number of men in cavalry companies varied, but on average was around 100–200, drawn up in ranks of 4 to 5 men deep.[15]

After a quick reconnaissance of the positions occupied by the Archduke, Condé ordered his troops to halt. The French were positioned on a ridge, opposite Loos and Grenay and near to the Béthune road, with their left flank on the La Bassée road, and the right flank opposite Liévin. Condé set up his command post in an area close to his right wing, from where he could see the whole battlefield.[16]

Ottavio Piccolomini (1599–1656), engraving dated 1649. Piccolomini was born in Florence and at the age of 16 was a pikeman in an Italian company in the service of Spain. In 1618 he was promoted to the rank of captain and given command of a company of cavalry which the Grand Duke of Tuscany sent to The Emperor to fight against the Bohemian rebels. He took part in the Battle of the White Mountain (1620) and in the campaigns of the beginning of the Thirty Years' War. In 1627 he joined Wallenstein's Army, rising to the rank of colonel. He returned to Italy on family business, but was recalled to Germany when the King of Sweden landed in Pomerania. In the 1630s he rose to importance as a high commander in the Imperial army, taking part in all fronts of the war. When the Imperial commander Peter Melander, was killed at the Battle at Zusmarshausen in May 1648, Piccolomini was appointed lieutenant-general to The Emperor (*Generalissimo*). (Public Domain)

---

12   According to Hardy, the main battle line included 10 battalions and 13 squadrons in the front line, then 6 battalions and 2 squadrons in reserve. Hardy, *Batailles Françaises*, p.104.

13   Aumale, *Histoire des Princes de Condé*, p.235. According to Hardy, there were 23 squadrons. Hardy, *Batailles Françaises*, p.103.

14   Godley, *The Great Condé*, p.219; Hardy, *Batailles Françaises*, p.104.

15   Guthrie, *Batallas de la Guerra de los Treinta Años*, p.296.

16   Aumale, *Histoire des Princes de Condé*, p 240.

Soon all the heights were crowned with smoke: the Spanish artillery was firing[17] and the first bullets hit the companies of the *Gardes*.[18]

The Spanish artillery was further away than the effective range of the French guns, so *Monsieur* de Cossé advanced with his light guns, escorted by Arnault's Carabins and firing from closer, although uphill, they engaged in an artillery duel, in which the French gunners shot much better than their Spanish opponents.[19] Cavalry skirmishers from both sides were sent to the centre of the plain, to scout out their opponent and these horsemen exchanged fire.[20] The Archduke's Croats, impatient to engage, rode against the French line, but were not supported by the regular squadrons of the Lorrainer or Walloon units, and so the Croats had to retreat.[21]

Both commanders-in-chief studied the battle order of the enemy army's units and considered their own.[22] Condé realised that he could not launch his army into a frontal assault on such an advantageous position as the enemy occupied. Time passed and no order to fight was given from either commander. On the plain, men and animals were standing in the summer heat, suffering from thirst and hunger. Some staff officers informed Condé of the state of the troops and suggested to him to withdraw the army to near Béthune, so that for a few hours at least men and horses would be able to rest, eat, and drink from the stream of Noeux, but Condé refused.[23]

However, in the afternoon, Condé changed his mind and in the area of Noeux, around 11 kilometres back, a camp could be set up from where the enemy force could still be observed, and where supplies and equipment could be distributed.[24] Condé was aware of the strength of the Spanish position at dawn on 19 August, reflecting that it would be madness to attack frontally with 16,000 men and 18 light cannon, against natural and artificial entrenchments

---

17   In the late afternoon, frightened peasants arrived in Arras and informed the Governor, *Monsieur* de La Tour, that the French army had deployed in front of the Spanish but that Condé had not dared to attack them. The Governor had also heard the cannon fire, so the garrison was on alert on the ramparts. Following the news from the peasants, he kept his garrison in place during the night. The next day, when the battle commenced, La Tour and his troops remained expectant, paying careful attention to the news that reached them throughout the day. Aumale, *Histoire des Princes de Condé*, p.240.

18   Hardy, *Batailles Françaises*, p.106.

19   Malo, *Champs de Bataille*, p.72.

20   Aumale, *Histoire des Princes de Condé*, p.240.

21   Hardy, *Batailles Françaises*, p.106.

22   Aumale, *Histoire des Princes de Condé*, p.240; Godley, *The Great Condé*, p.220.

23   Aumale, *Histoire des Princes de Condé*, p.239.

24   Godley, *The Great Condé*, p.220; BNH, Mss. 2379, 'Sucesos', f.198; According to Gramont:

      ...The Prince saw that there was no fodder or water where they were, so he decided to go to *Neus*, a village two leagues from where he was camped, to get provisions and food from Béthune, and thus be in a position to follow the enemy wherever they went.

      Thion, *Les Armées Françaises*, p.161.

      For Malo, the decision was taken under pressure from the officers and men:

      But in the afternoon, the French made complaints that the command could not help but worry: men and horses were dying of thirst in the middle of this arid plain, and the generals proposed a slight movement to the west, so to bring the troops closer to the stream of Noeux coming down from the high hills of Artois, which dominate the plain of Lens to the south.

      Malo, *Champs de Bataille*, p.70.

defended by 20,000 men with 38 guns.[25] Moreover, the French Army could not continue to just wait on that arid, sun-scorched plain, where there was neither water nor fodder.[26]

Hardy says that Béthune was the likely destination, and the French could arrive there and rest before the end of the day. Condé explained his plan:

> If the enemy descends from his heights to attack the marching army, so much the better! We will turn around and fight in less disadvantageous conditions; moving is not running away! We will move to the left to march towards the right; the direction will be the village of Noeux, on the road from Arras to Béthune. The Compte d'Erlach will start the movement with the 6 Weimarian squadrons of the reserve. The left wing, the main body and the artillery, formed in as many columns as lines, will follow in succession, under the protection of the right wing, which will form the rearguard. The squadrons and battalions will keep their distances and intervals. If we halt, it will be to form up in battle, facing the enemy, on the right or half turn, in the formation of the previous day.[27]

The question now was in which moment Condé would give the order to retreat: the prudent thing to do was to move at night, which was much safer but which, in practice, presented enormous problems of coordination between units in moving towards the camp. Moving by day was more dignified, more orderly, but more risky, as it would expose their movement and the enemy would not miss the opportunity to attack.[28]

Condé chose to move by day; French historiography argues that he did so to maintain his prestige. Gramont, who was part of Condé's inner circle, claimed that the Prince made this decision to show the enemy that he was not afraid of them. Given the final result of the battle, this may be considered a wise move; but had the result been otherwise, much would be made of the error of having made this tactical move in full view of the enemy, and whether it would not have been better to have made it at night, even with the difficulties that may have involved.[29]

Gramont, a first-hand witness, states: 'and as he wished to show them his desire to fight, and that he was not afraid of them, he withdrew from his position in front of them in broad daylight.'[30]

Gramont's words are revealing; Condé was very reserved in expressing his thoughts, both to maintain his prestige, the distance between his junior officers and, especially, to prevent

French infantry officers. From the engraving depicting the siege of Philippsburg in 1644. (Riksarkivet, Stockholm)

---

25 Thion, *Les Armées Françaises*, p.160.

26 Hardy, *Batailles Françaises*, p.107; Quincy, *Histoire Militaire*, p.97.

27 Hardy, *Batailles Françaises*, p.107.

28 Godley, *The Great Condé*, p.220.

29 Wilson affirms that 'It was obvious the Spanish position was too strong and he [Condé] began to retreat'; for Wilson, then, Condé's initial decision was simply to avoid launching a frontal attack on a well-defended position. Wilson: *Europe's Tragedy*, p.507.

30 Thion, *Les Armées Françaises*, p.161.

Spanish spies from discovering his intentions; perhaps his only confidence was with Gramont.[31]

As it was getting dark, Condé gave the order to bivouac in the field, some distance behind where they were, to prevent any night attack by the enemy, by contrast the Spanish could sleep in their camp. That night, the Spanish sent the Croat regiment to skirmish against the French, but when they approached the French positions they saw that French artillery was in position and strong guards watched over the camp, so the Croats quickly returned to the Spanish lines.[32]

Soldiers camping in the field, Peter Snayers (1592–1667), dated between 1612 and 1667. Snayers has illustrated an everyday situation for troops in the field. In a village, soldiers are talking in a relaxed manner, in groups, infantry and horsemen. Note particularly the high proportion of firearms among all the soldiers, as well as the lack of uniformity of them, wearing clothing of many different colours. This is a Spanish force, as can be seen from the red scarfs. (Metropolitan Museum of Art, New York, MET DT340534)

The morning of the 20th, the troops formed up and the march, actually a tactical retreat, began, and to show the enemy that they were not sneaking away, Condé waited until the sun had risen and ordered Cossé to fire a

---

31 Godley, *The Great Condé*, p.221.
32 Thion, *Les Armées Françaises*, p.165.

barrage from six artillery pieces to alert the enemy army.[33] In the withdrawal, the previous order of march was reversed: Erlach's reserve now went first; the troops that had formed the left flank moved next, followed by the units of the centre. Being the rearguard was now the responsibility of the troops that had formed the French right flank.[34]

Châtillon, with the cavalry of the centre, was ready to support the rearguard. If the Archduke decided to attack, he would not catch the French Army unawares.[35]

These orders were clearly and precisely given to the assembled generals before setting out; the movement was begun at about six o'clock in the morning. Condé, surrounded by the officers and *gentilshomme* of his personal retinue – Boutteville, Marans, Bellefontaine, La Peyrère, Normanville and Lafont – took up position on the right flank, to watch the retreat of his army and observe the reaction of the Spanish Army.[36] The army, to retreat towards Noeux, was to follow an east-northeast direction, with the line of retreat along the plateau between Grenay and Mazingarbe. The movement was to begin with an oblique change of front, which placed the army perpendicular to its line of retreat.[37]

Obviously, the movement of the French Army did not go unnoticed by the Spanish. Beck, from the hill of Liévin where his infantry was stationed, saw the movement of the French, and galloped to inform the Archduke, saying '*Monsieur* the Prince is escaping. You must go after him!'[38]

But the Archduke was a cautious man: he feared a feint, and ordered the infantry battalions not to move, however he acceded to Beck's request for some offensive action: 'Let the Croats skirmish if it pleases Beck and let the Lorraine squadrons support them, as they are closer to those fleeing.'[39]

The French Army's march was proceeding smoothly when the Croat cavalry squadrons appeared near the French rear. Condé ordered the regiment *Son Altesse Royale* to stop them. The leading Croat squadron fell on the French regiment and broke it up, and its *mestre de camp* Brancas was wounded and captured.[40] The rest of the Lorraine squadrons then attacked and overran the remaining men of the *Son Altesse Royale* regiment.

Noirmoutiers led 6 other regiments and engaged in skirmishing against the Croats; but the Lorrainer cavalry, 'the most feared in Europe' according to Hardy, also came into action and defeated Noirmoutiers' horsemen.[41]

33   Thion, *Les Armées Françaises*, p.165.
34   Thion, *Les Armées Françaises*, p.161; Quincy, *Histoire Militaire*, p.97.
35   Godley, *The Great Condé*, p.221.
36   Hardy, *Batailles Françaises*, p.107.
37   Aumale, *Histoire des Princes de Condé*, p.241.
38   Hardy, *Batailles Françaises*, p.108.
39   Hardy, *Batailles Françaises*, p.108.
40   Aumale, *Histoire des Princes de Condé*, p.241; Desormeaux, *Histoire de Louis de Borbon*, tome 1, p.68; Hardy, *Batailles Françaises*, p.108; Montglat, *Collection des Mémoires*, p.99. Gramont affirms that cavalry of Lorraine, captained by Beck, were those who defeated Brancas' detachment. Thion, *Les Armées Françaises*, p.161.
41   Hardy, *Batailles Françaises*, p.108.

THE BATTLE OF LENS 1648

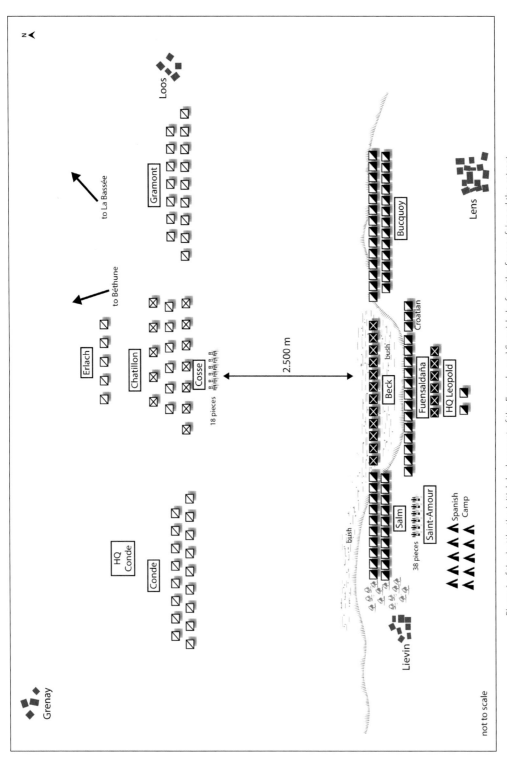

Phase 1 of the battle: the initial deployment of the French, and Spanish, before the former feigned the retreat.

This map shows the deployment of the two armies. The French march into the open field with the uneasiness of knowing that the enemy is close. The Spanish and their allies control the heights and wait patiently for the enemy to approach.

Condé deploys his army with cavalry on both flanks; As is usual with him, he reserves command of the more powerful cavalry on the right; this battle formation suggests that he wishes to overwhelm the enemy's flank and surround them.

Condé ordered Châtillon to bring up the reserve, the 6 squadrons of the *Gendarmerie de France*.[42] The Duc de Châtillon left it to the *sergents de bataille* to direct the infantry's march and he took command of the horsemen.[43] They turned left in line, in order, following their standards at a trot. Hardy described the French counter-attack: 'Never was a more beautiful charge seen, nor made with better grace!'[44] Châtillon's charge to stop the Lorrainer cavalry avalanche was effective and they pushed the enemy back up the hill from which they had descended, but the Lorrainer General, Ligniville, reorganised the fugitives, and with the support of three large squadrons of reinforcements to support the Croats and Lorrainers, again charged the French, and the French counter-attack was beaten.[45] The French *gendarmes* squadrons were split in two and scattered right and left.[46] Some French cavalry tried to withdraw in order, but were supported only by the Picardy infantry regiment, which was on the right flank of the front line.[47]

Condé, who had foreseen the disorder, had planned two things: one, that the troops going to Noeux should draw up on the next height (between Aix and Grenay), and the other, that the second line of the right wing should halt and fight on the plain to cover the retreat from Châtillon. Condé had given the order to the Gassion cavalry regiment: 'Remember Rocroi!'[48]

Jean, Comte de Gassion (1609–1647), nineteenth century engraving after the portrait by Jean Alaux (1786–1864), painted in 1835, on display at Versailles. From an early age, Gassion's destiny was to become a soldier. He served in all the European theatres of war and had a well-deserved reputation for bravery and intelligence. The *Gazette de France* turned him into a hero for the general public, intertwining true stories with the adventures of the journalists' invention. On 28 September 1647, during an inspection at the siege of Lens, he was shot in the head with a musket ball, from which he died in Arras on 2 October. (Public Domain)

42   Batailles, 1696, p.210; Hardy, *Batailles Françaises*, p.108; Quincy, *Histoire Militaire*, p.98.
43   Aumale, *Histoire des Princes de Condé*, p.241.
44   Hardy, *Batailles Françaises*, p.108.
45   Hardy, *Batailles Françaises*, p.108.
46   Aumale, *Histoire des Princes de Condé*, p.242; Godley, *The Great Condé*, p.221.
47   Thion, *Les Armées Françaises*, p.165.
48   Hardy, *Batailles Françaises*, p.108.

Cavalry fight. Jan Martszen de Jonge, between 1619 and 1649 (Rijksmuseum, Amsterdam)

The commanding officer of the *Régiment* de Gassion was Guillaume de La Villette, who sent his squadrons into the charge,[49] but as they approached the line of battle, the disorganised *gendarmes* caused the Gassion horsemen to lose their cohesion; some of them were afraid of facing the fearsome Croats and Lorrainers, so they turned away. Disorder began to spread among the Gassion cavalry. Condé encouraged his men to hold their ground, but the momentum of the Lorrainers was too strong and panic spread through the ranks of the French cavalry. Condé's efforts were futile. The Lorrainers were advancing too fast and Condé had to be dragged back by his officers.[50] He

---

49 Malo describes this action as:

> ... Both troops march against each other. At 100 paces, the Lorrainers set off at a trot .... The enemy, astonished, halted; we were 10 paces away, with pistol raised. Our troops halt; everyone's eyes are fixed on *Monsieur le Prince* who is in front, between the two squadrons of Villette; he can count on this regiment: it was Gassion's regiment. The Prince de Salm is in front of him.

> After a few moments' hesitation, the Lorrainers send a general volley. Many of our men are on the ground; but Condé's sword is drawn and gleams in the sun: it is the signal. 'Remember Rocroy', he shouts to Gassion's veteran soldiers.

> With swords and pistols, our horsemen close in on the Prince of Salm's; the front line of the enemy is broken. *Monsieur* de Ligniville was a little further back; he purposefully launches eight squadrons that check the onslaught of ours. In turn, *Monsieur le Prince*, who, at the first blow, has resumed his responsibility as leader, calls up his second line and sends it forward; it was the squadrons that turned back in the morning; Condé takes the lead, and this time they follow bravely, regaining lost ground.

> Malo, *Champs de Bataille*, p.73.

50 Godley, *The Great Condé*, p.222.

barely escaped thanks 'only to the speed and vigour of his horse;'[51] his page was not so lucky and was wounded in the fight.[52]

The next line of defence for the French was at the foot of the Grenay Heights where their left wing was stationed with the infantry and the reserve of the Count d'Erlach.[53]

Hardy relates that, 'those who had kept their wits about them in their flight stopped before a ravine on the plain.'[54] It was there that Condé rallied and regrouped many of his cavalry, put them back into ranks and waited for the onslaught of the Lorrainer and Croat horsemen.

Ligniville was exultant, for he had destroyed the body of enemy cavalry; but the veteran general was not foolish, when he saw the French main body begin to deploy, he did not attempt a further charge, which would have been suicidal, but ordered his squadrons to withdraw and to fall back to the hill of Loos, which they did in good order. Here the rest of the army awaited them.[55]

At that moment, when part of the French cavalry was in disarray and the rest of the army was deploying and reorienting its front, the Spanish did not attack. Condé was puzzled that Leopold did not take advantage of these moments of disarray to attack. Those precious minutes were used by Condé to reorganise his forces, with his cavalry reformed and his infantry drawing up on the Height of Grenay. The French had fallen back around 2,000 metres, halting on the crest of a similar hill to the one they had occupied in the morning – at the same level and with the same orientation. The line of the French army was no more than 1,800 metres, with the village of Grenay to the rear of their right, that of Loos some distance in front of their left.[56]

While the units were sorting themselves out, Condé redrew his battle plan: the cavalry units' defeat severely weakened them, so they could no longer be suitable as shock troops; the second line of cavalry on the right wing would become the first; the two lines countermarched and passed through each other. The surviving *gendarmes* returned to their original position between the two lines of infantry. Condé ordered the regiments to be reminded of his initial orders: advance in line, at a slow pace, and wait for the enemy salvo to be returned with a very heavy volley of fire.[57]

Beck, from his position, had witnessed the charges of the Spanish cavalry, brilliantly led by the Prince de Salm and the Lorrainers Lignéville and Clinchamp. He had seen the French *Gendarmerie's* fighting retreat, so he rode up to the Archduke's command post, and 'with his pride born of German swagger,'[58] asserted that, 'we had only to descend to the plain to find there the dazzling revenge of Rocroi, to annihilate these accursed French, to

---

51   Aumale, *Histoire des Princes de Condé*, p.242; Hardy, *Batailles Françaises*, p.109.

52   Thion, *Les Armées Françaises*, p.161.

53   Hardy, *Batailles Françaises*, p.109.

54   Hardy, *Batailles Françaises*, p.109.

55   Aumale, *Histoire des Princes de Condé*, p.243; Godley, *The Great Condé*, p.222; Hardy, *Batailles Françaises*, p.109.

56   Aumale, *Histoire des Princes de Condé*, p.246.

57   Godley, *The Great Condé*, p.222; Hardy, *Batailles Françaises*, p.110.

58   Thion, *Les Armées Françaises*, p.161.

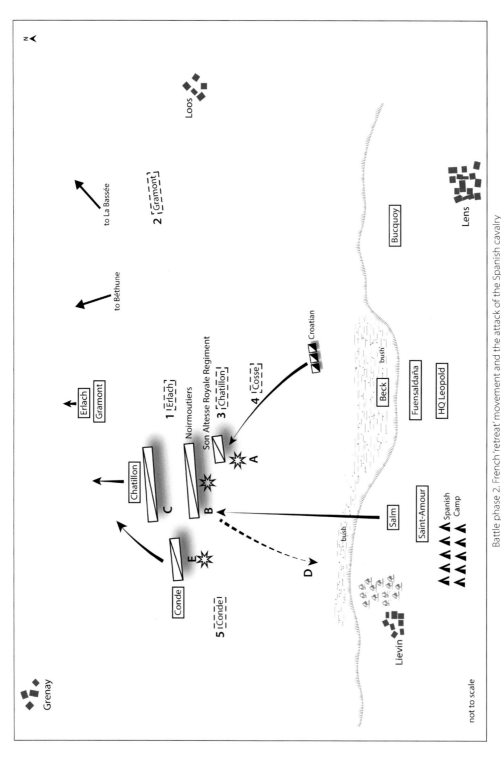

Battle phase 2. French 'retreat' movement and the attack of the Spanish cavalry

Condé orders a tactical retreat to more advantageous positions to rest the French army. The withdrawal begins with order and without setback; the order of march in the retreat will be as follows: 1 Erlach, 2 Gramont, 3 Chatillon, 4 Cossé-Brissac and 5 Condé. But General Beck considers that it is an ideal opportunity to attack and partially manages to convince the Archduke to order an attack: first the Croatian cavalry launch and then the Lorraine cavalry. Some detachments of French horsemen try to cut off this advance (A), but they cannot and little by little more French cavalry joins in (B); meanwhile, the rest of the French army manages to distance itself and redeploy. Chatillon with his horsemen finally manages to repel the enemy attack (C) and the Lorrainese retreat (D), but their reserve helps them regroup and they launch a new cavalry attack. Condé leads a counterattack but fails and has to flee hastily to avoid being captured (E).

French and Spanish cavalry clash during the Battle of Lens in 1648. Pieter Nolpe, 1648 (Rijksmuseum, Amsterdam)

capture the Bourbon and send them all, in chains, to Brussels, so that they could dictate peace to the Regent.[59]

Leopold was persuaded and gave the order to attack the French.[60] The cavalry of the Prince of Salm opened up on the right and left to give way to the rest of the Spanish Army, led by the Archduke, who had advanced from their initial position in front of the walls of Lens.[61]

After a while, the Spanish line came over the ridge; they were also at a slow, cautious pace. Beck rode up to the Archduke and asked him to ride forward with him, to show him that the French infantry had been left unprotected, with no cavalry to protect them, on completely flat ground. It was tempting to attack this infantry, but the Archduke affirmed that he had given express orders that no risk was to be taken. Beck insisted that there was no risk and offered his head as a symbol of his belief in victory. Beck felt guilty for the defeat at Rocroi, and felt that the Spanish officers and soldiers blamed him

---

59 Aumale, *Histoire des Princes de Condé*, p.244; Hardy, *Batailles Françaises*, p.110.

60 Cánovas del Castillo indicates that Fuensaldaña was opposed to leaving the dominant position they held and that the Archduke's justification for ordering an advance of the army was that he did not want to leave the cavalry that had attacked and defeated the French cavalry unprotected. Antonio Cánovas del Castillo, *Obras Completas*, (Madrid: Fundación Cánovas del Castillo, 1997), p.654.

61 Hardy, *Batailles Françaises*, p.111.

for it; now Beck believed that the time had come to redeem himself and make up for Rocroi with the victory at Lens against the Prince of Condé.[62]

According to Beck, all that was left to do was to make one more attack and victory would be theirs; he thought the French would put up little resistance, but he was wrong – the French had no intention of leaving.

While all of this was going on in the front line, the captain of *Maréchal* de Gramont's Guard informed Gramont that the French rearguard had been defeated and was in disarray, and that this, 'did not bode well'. With this news, Gramont ordered his troops, marching in order of battle to turn back, leaving only a small body of 30 cavalry behind the squadrons. This done, he rode at full gallop to the place where the Prince of Condé was stationed.[63]

Meanwhile, the Prince reviewed his troops and harangued them: 'His presence, his words and the joy he showed on his face inspired new enthusiasm in the soldiers.'[64] Far from being discouraged, he was exultant,[65] foreseeing that the decisive moment of the battle would soon come. He rode through the ranks of the soldiers and encouraged them to fight and to have courage:

> My friends, pluck up your courage. You will all have to fight today; there will be no use in turning back, for I promise you that all shall serve alike; the brave men of their own free will, and the cowards because there will be no escape.[66]

While the soldiers acclaimed their general, Gramont approached Condé and the Prince hugged him and said it that he was annoyed at the hasty retreat of some moments ago and he complained about the behaviour of some of the French cavalry.[67] He added that he was particularly pained that its own regiment had abandoned him shamefully. The conversation that they had was of short duration, 'knowing very well that on such occasions a long discussion is neither careful nor wise.'[68]

Then, the Prince de Condé told *Maréchal* Gramont that he needed time to put the second line in the position of the first, because he was afraid that the latter would probably be defeated if he pushed it once more into a charge. Gramont wrote:

> This knowledge that he [Condé] had about men is what always put him above other [men] on the most dangerous occasions; because everything that he had to do came to him in an instant. Such men have a rare genius for war, a type of which there is only one in a hundred thousand.[69]

---

62 Hardy, *Batailles Françaises,* p.111; Montglat, *Collection des Mémoires,* p.100; Thion, *Les Armées Françaises,* p.165.
63 Thion, *Les Armées Françaises,* p.161.
64 Hardy, *Batailles Françaises,* p.110.
65 Godley, *The Great Condé,* p.223.
66 Godley, *The Great Condé,* p.223.
67 Aumale, *Histoire des Princes de Condé,* p.243.
68 Thion, *Les Armées Françaises,* p.161.
69 Thion, *Les Armées Françaises,* p.161.

Spanish Army of Flanders, Gentleman Cavalry Trooper

Reconstruction based on a series of paintings showing the clothing of Spanish soldiers of the period by many of the most famous artists of the era, such as Jusepe, Rizi, Fray Juan Andrés, Snayers and Vrancx. The trooper is armed with a sword and shown holding one of a pair of wheellock pistols. He displays his loyalty in the red military scarf widely used throughout all Habsburg Armies. (*Illustration by Sergey Shemnkov © Helion & Company 2025*)

Spanish Army of Flanders, veteran pikeman

Based on images of Spanish soldiers from the 1630s, but especially a pikeman shown by the little-known Spanish artist Félix Castello (Madrid, 1595-1651). The pikeman's clothing is fashionably of the period and he wears decorated breeches but a plain, functional leather coat, called a *cuera* in Spanish, very common in both infantry and cavalry; This garment provided some protection against sword cuts. (*Illustration by Sergey Shemnkov © Helion & Company 2025*)

French Musketeer, 1646–1647

Based on Lostelneau's *Le Maréchal de Bataille*. Musketeers were armed with a musket with 12 charges of powder, and a sword. (*Illustration by Giorgio Albertini © Helion & Company 2025*)

Chevau-léger Officer c. 1640–1643

Based on a painting *Halt of Bohemians and Soldiers*, by Sebastien Bourdon in the Musée Fabre, Montpellier. French officers wore a scarf, generally white, to distinguish themselves and proclaim their allegiance to the French Crown. (*Illustration by Giorgio Albertini © Helion & Company 2025*)

It had been more than 2 hours since Condé had given the order of withdrawing towards the camp, at dawn.[70] It seemed like an eternity. It was now nearly 8 in the morning, and it appeared that the sought-for battle had started.

Condé gave his orders to the rest of his generals. They all knew what to do:

> *Monsieur le Prince* had already given his orders: everything having been considered beforehand: everyone's place, the general movement [of the army], the detailed procedures. A single word of command was all that was needed.[71]

At the other end of the battlefield, Gramont met with his troops. Close to his position was a small village, which limited the space Condé could use to deploy his troops as he planned. This forced Gramont to retreat slightly to the left up to three times, and to move his troops to higher ground; he then redeployed his troops for battle.[72]

Condé was aware that, in his haste to give battle, the Archduke was abandoning his advantageous positions on the hill. He is reputed to have said to his entourage: 'Since the Archduke has left an impregnable position to attack us, it is now up to us to win or die! Forward!'[73]

According to Hardy, Condé's ruse had succeeded: his retreat had only been a feint to engage the enemy in battle, to encourage them to abandon their positions and advance towards the plain. Condé was ready, Leopold was not; the French had hurried to put themselves in order, to surprise the Spaniards in disarray as they charged them.[74]

So it was 8 o'clock in the morning when the two armies advanced their lines to open the battle. The Spanish were somewhat hasty, while the French Army began to advance slowly towards the Spanish lines, to the sound of trumpets, drums and cannon. Despite Condé's order to advance in line and keep their spacing, every now and then a unit would move out of line, so Condé had to halt the march to reorganise the line. According to the account of General La Peyrère, Cossé's artillery was so well trained that they were able

Henri de La Ferté-Senneterre, *Maréchal*-Duc de La Ferté (1599–1681), unknown engraver. La Ferté-Senneterre's family tradition was one of service to the State: his father was an ambassador and politician, and his grandfather a soldier. La Ferté-Senneterre entered a military career at a very young age, serving The Netherlands in its war of independence against Spain (the Eighty Years' War). In 1628 he was a captain at the siege of La Rochelle and rose through the military ranks: *Mestre de camp, Maréchal de camp, Lieutenant Général* and finally *Maréchal de France*. As a reward for his record of service and loyalty to the Crown, in 1665 Louis XIV elevated the marquisate of La Ferté-Senneterre to the dignity of a duchy. (Public Domain)

---

70   Aumale, *Histoire des Princes de Condé*, p.246.
71   Aumale, *Histoire des Princes de Condé*, p.245.
72   Thion, *Les Armées Françaises*, p.161.
73   Hardy, *Batailles Françaises,* p.111; Godley, *The Great Condé*, p.223.
74   Hardy, *Batailles Françaises,* p.111.

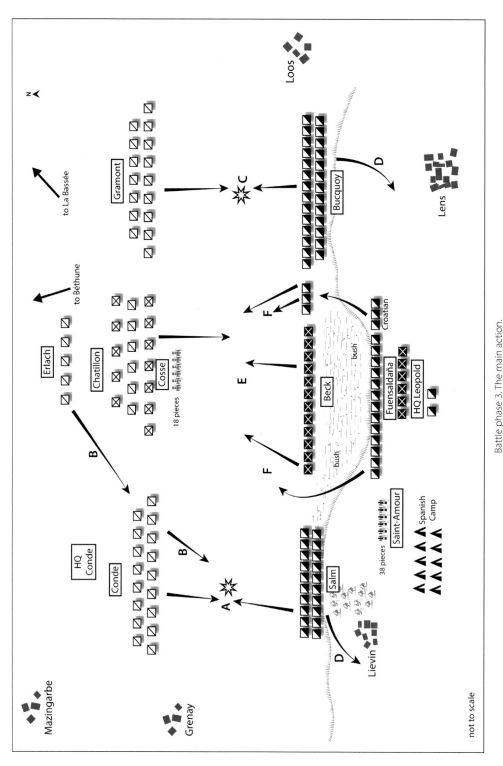

Battle phase 3. The main action.

The two armies approach; the battles take place almost simultaneously, but we narrate them sequentially: Condé's horsemen and Salm's Lorraine men confront each other (A); then Erlach's reserve cavalry arrives (B) and Condé achieves victory at that point. On the other flank, after hard fighting (C), Gramont's cavalry defeats Bucquoy's Walloon cavalry: the two Spanish cavalry retreat (D). In the centre, the two infantry advance and clash (E); initially the French seem to win, but Beck takes advantage of the gaps in the French line and launches himself with the rest of his troops; in addition, riders from Fuensaldaña's reserve join the combat (F), conquering the French artillery. Chatillon launches a counterattack and recovers the cannons and the centre of the battle.

to fire on the move.'[75] And when firing from the plain to the hill where the enemy was, all the shots hit the cavalry squadrons and the infantry battalions.[76]

When the two great opposing lines of infantry were at a distance of about 30 paces, 'a stone's throw away', 3 volleys were fired from the Spanish left wing. Condé ordered his line to halt and reminded them of the order that the Spanish were to fire first.[77]

This was a wise and sensible order from Condé for three reasons: it tempered the ardour of the troops; it allowed the lines to be readjusted; and it confirmed to the ordinary soldiers the determination of their general of the importance of withstanding the onslaught of the enemy.[78]

For their part, the Spanish front-line battalions, under the command of Prince de Salm, were also ordered to halt. A few moments passed in which both armies remained silent and still, waiting for the other to attack.[79]

While the French halted their entire line, the Prince de Salm advanced at a trot, with the first line of Walloon and Lorrainer cavalry, against Condé's cavalry line, formed by 7 squadrons, who advanced to meet them.[80] The two lines of cavalry approached each other, but stopped just a few metres apart:

Armoured pikeman. Salomon Savery, between 1635 and 1655. Note the helmet slung at the back of his back plate, the hook to do so is clearly visible. (Stephen Ede-Borrett collection)

> The ranks rest with horse head against horse head, muzzle against muzzle, and remain in this position for a long time, awaiting, without moving to either side, to see who would fire first.[81]

It was the Spanish cavalry that gave in to their nerves first and were the first to fire. The near point-blank volley caused heavy casualties among the French, especially among the officers, 'It was as if the gates of hell had opened. All our front-line officers were shot down, killed or wounded.'[82]

Condé, after the Spanish volley, gave the order to fire to his infantry. And himself, with sword in hand and followed by the other 6 squadrons charged the Spaniards. The French impetus was such that they broke through Salm's first line.[83]

But such impetus was met by the second Spanish cavalry line formed by the Lorrainers, who stopped and drove back the victorious French. In the bloody mêlée, Villequier was dismounted and La Moussaye wounded – both

75   Thion, *Les Armées Françaises*, p.163.

76   Aumale, *Histoire des Princes de Condé*, p.247; Hardy, *Batailles Françaises*, p.111.

77   Hardy, *Batailles Françaises*, p.112; Godley, *The Great Condé*, p.223; Thion, *Les Armées Françaises*, p.163.

78   Hardy, *Batailles Françaises*, p.112; Thion, *Les Armées Françaises*, p.163.

79   Godley, *The Great Condé*, p.224; Thion, *Les Armées Françaises*, p.163.

80   Hardy, *Batailles Françaises*, p.112.

81   Hardy, *Batailles Françaises*, p.112.

82   Thion, *Les Armées Françaises*, p.163.

83   Aumale, *Histoire des Princes de Condé*, p.248; Godley, *The Great Condé*, p.224; Hardy, *Batailles Françaises*, p.112.

Spanish infantry during the siege of La Bassée in 1642. Petrus Rucholle, 1642 (Rijksmuseum, Amsterdam)

were captured:[84] General La Moussaye was found wounded under his dead horse and was hurried away from the battlefield to Lens; General Villequier was taken prisoner by General Ligniville himself – Ligniville was in the habit of seeking out and confronting opposing generals. Villequier was also taken to Lens.[85]

Condé ordered Noirmoutiers, with the second line, to advance and to attack Ligniville, who advanced with his cavalry to cover the gap that Salm had left. For the next hour bitter fighting continued on both sides.[86]

Condé understood that the crisis of the battle had been reached; the French Prince appeared to be everywhere – giving orders, encouraging his men; the chroniclers described him as having 'superhuman' energy. 'Condé passed like lightning from one place to another and it would seem that he was everywhere at the same time.'[87]

Condé brought forward his reserve, the German squadrons of the Count of Erlach. The Prince of Salm countered with his Lorrainer cavalry, led by Lignéville; however, the Lorrainer reserve had already fought that morning and men and mounts were tired, and Erlach's horsemen won the engagement. The defeat of the Lorrainers led to the defeat of the whole of the Archduke's left wing.[88] Malo credits Erlach himself with the initiative to attack:

84 Hardy, *Batailles Françaises,* p.113; Montglat, *Collection des Mémoires,* p.100.
85 Aumale, *Histoire des Princes de Condé,* p.248; Malo, 1899, p.73.
86 Godley, *The Great Condé,* p.224.
87 Hardy, *Batailles Françaises,* p.113. For Godley, the Prince de Condé charged 10 times. Godley, *The Great Condé,* p.224. In any case, regardless of the exact number of times, everything indicates Condé's valour in the battle, but also that this was a very hard fight and that the battle was very close for both sides; certainly not as easy a victory for the French as later accounts claim.
88 Aumale, *Histoire des Princes de Condé,* p.248; Hardy, *Batailles Françaises,* p.113.

d'Erlach had correctly judged the importance of the fight on our right flank. When he saw Lorraine's cavalry flank the Prince's cavalry for a moment and attempt to envelop it, he immediately broke off, marched to his right, and, reforming to the left in line, took position on the flank of the fight.[89]

On the flank commanded by Gramont,[90] when the *maréchal* had deployed his troops, he positioned himself at the head of his men and told them that the battle was about to be decided, that they should remember the courage shown on previous occasions, to remember what they owed to the King, and to pay close attention to the orders given to them. He said that this imminent action was of such importance, given the present state of the battle, that there were only two options – victory or death, and that he himself was going to show them the way, and be the first in action against the enemy squadrons to their front. Gramont said that the Walloons would meet them with a volley, but that the French would then have the great advantage in the fight. The troops shouted enthusiastically: the infantry threw their hats in the air, while the cavalry waved their swords above their heads, and the musicians sounded their trumpets and drums.[91]

Gramont charged at the head of the Mazarin regiment, leading with the 9 front-line squadrons, and accompanied by the Marquis de Saint-Mégrin and Compte de Lillebonne.

Maréchal Gramont was facing the Walloon cavalry near the village of Loos, under the command of the Conde de Bucquoy, who led the first line, and the Prince de Ligne in the second.[92] The Walloon called this type of cavalry *compagnies franches*, heavy cavalry riders, well armed, but well mounted, well exercised; these units were known in other armies as 'cuirassiers',[93] but in the Spanish military terminology they were 'horses-cuirasses' (*Caballos-coraza*). The Walloon cavalry was located on a small hill. In Gramont's words, 'it can be said that it was a duel more than a battle, since each squadron and battalion had its counterpart to fight.'[94]

The Walloon cavalry stayed stationary, with the advantage of the higher ground; it was five or six paces behind the ridge. The position was well chosen: if the French came up the hill, they would arrive tired and in disarray, while the Walloon cavalry, formed and waiting, could charge them in order. The

89 Malo, *Champs de Bataille*, p.74. Aumale and Guthrie also consider that the action of attacking the Lorrainers' flank was Erlach's own initiative (Aumale, *Histoire des Princes de Condé*, p.253; Guthrie, *Batallas de la Guerra de los Treinta Años*, p.295).

90 For the historian Malo, Gramont must have acted earlier, perhaps simultaneously with Condé's attack:
    However diligent he may have been in observing the order given and maintaining the general alignment, Gramont had not been able to come to blows as soon as *Monsieur le Prince*
    Malo, *Champs de Bataille*, p.73.

91 Thion, *Les Armées Françaises*, p.161.

92 Aumale, *Histoire des Princes de Condé*, p.248; Malo, *Champs de Bataille*, p.73; Quincy, *Histoire Militaire*, p.98; Thion, *Les Armées Françaises*, p.162.

93 Malo, *Champs de Bataille*, p.73.

94 Thion, *Les Armées Françaises*, p.162.

Cavalry from the later phase of the Thirty Years' War, when buff coats often replaced the iron back and breast previously common. Jan Martszen de Jonge, between 1619 and 1649 (Rijksmuseum, Amsterdam)

Walloon cavalry on that flank awaited not with sword in hand, but armed with, as their primary weapon, short arquebuses.[95]

The French, after climbing the slope without breaking formation, were indeed greeted with a furious volley; Gramont himself says that 'this discharge was so close range and so terrible that it could have been said that hell opened.'[96] After the volley there were barely any officers in charge of the French squadrons surviving. But despite these casualties, the French cavalry broke the first line of Walloon cavalry, just as Gramont had predicted, and caused them many casualties.[97]

However, a French squadron from Gramont's detachment, ascending the steepest part of the hill, was thrown back by a Spanish detachment, which pursued fast and charged into the flank of the Persan infantry battalion. The infantry regiment, with its *mestre de camp* François de Vaudetar, Marquis de Persan, barely held out against such an unexpected attack. But La Ferté-Seneterre, who had just broken up the enemy squadrons on the ridge, seeing the danger, turned back with part of his cavalry and charged the enemy

---

95   Thion, *Les Armées Françaises*, p.162.
96   Thion, *Les Armées Françaises*, p.162.
97   Aumale, *Histoire des Princes de Condé*, p.250; Thion, *Les Armées Françaises*, p.162.

squadron, causing it to break and flee.[98] This Spanish force, in its flight back up the hill crashed into the other Spanish units massively disordering them.[99]

The second Walloon line, commanded by the Prince de Ligne, then advanced to support the first line, but was unable to break Gramont's troops, who had itself been reinforced with units from the second line. This reinforced body finally broke what was left of the Spanish right flank. Gramont, as was usual in his style of command, was brave and was fighting in the front line, and was on the verge of being captured on two or three occasions.[100]

Gramont recalled that one of the enemy squadrons that appeared to be fleeing fell upon his force at the moment when he least expected it, and that he would have been captured or killed had they not been in such a hurry to escape the field. While he found himself in the midst of the Spanish cavalry, an enemy trooper fired at him and his staff and killed one of his aides-de-camp who was beside him.[101]

While the cavalry combat was taking place on both flanks, the two lines of infantry moved into the fight. Beck led the Spanish, Germans and Walloons, Châtillon the French. The front ranks halted at 10 *toises* apart.[102] The two battalions of the *Gardes Françaises* were in the centre, on their right the *Gardes Suisses*, and on their left the *Gardes Écossaises*.[103]

The Landeszeughaus in Graz is considered the largest preserved historical armoury in the world, containing 32,000 pieces, including armour, firearms, polearms, swords, and cannon, dating from the fifteenth to the eighteenth century. This is a panoramic view of the room dedicated to armour: in the foreground, examples of cavalry armour, the kind used by cuirassiers, showing the near total protection that it offered. On the shelves on both sides are hundreds of infantry helmets (morions, cabassets, burgonets), breastplates and armour for pikemen and cavalry. (Author's photo)

98 Malo, *Champs de Bataille*, p.73.
99 Hardy, *Batailles Françaises*, p.114.
100 Hardy, *Batailles Françaises*, p.114.
101 Thion, *Les Armées Françaises*, p.162.
102 Aumale, *Histoire des Princes de Condé*, p.250; Hardy, *Batailles Françaises*, p.114; Thion, *Les Armées Françaises*, p.162. A *toise* would amount to about 2 m (https://en.wikipedia.org/wiki/Toise).
103 Aumale, *Histoire des Princes de Condé*, p.251; Hardy, *Batailles Françaises*, p.114.

Musketeer. He has a musket but of the newer lighter model and thus without a rest. The cap is probably an extravagant variation of the Montero. Salomon Savery, between 1635 and 1655. (Stephen Ede-Borrett collection)

Condé's order not to fire first was initially carried out; the musketeers had their weapons ready and waited. Suddenly the officers of the *Gardes Françaises*, impatient, raised their hats and shouted, 'Give Fire!'[104] A terrible volley, point-blank, killed and wounded the front ranks of the three Spanish regiments – one Spanish, two German – facing them. The French pikemen rushed forward and attacked the remainder of the Spanish troops; the Swiss followed the French example and aggressively charged, all of them getting well inside the Spanish lines.[105] This, however, now created a gap in the middle of the French lines.

Beck was an experienced general, took advantage of the fact that the *Gardes* were attacking the Spanish centre and ordered the Marqués de Bonifaz's and Bentivoglio's tercios attack through the gap, supported by some squadrons of cavalry. The move was very effective: the Spanish infantry took the French artillery, which was in the centre and had been left unprotected. Some *garde* units were surrounded, and took a large number of casualties.[106] The episode is described by Malo with emphasis on Beck's actions:

> The terrible Beck was watching them: he threw infantry and cavalry at these three battalions (for the Swiss Guard, in a spirit of brotherhood, had followed their comrades of the *Maison du Roi*). There has never been such a massacre. All the misfortune of the fight fell on the poor guards.[107]

The Spanish infantry continued their overwhelming advance and also destroyed the regiments of Nettancourt and Vaubecourt. The Spanish captured *Maréchal* d'Aumont but then killed him with a pistol shot, after he had already surrendered.[108]

Guthrie explains it differently:

> Four of the French front-line battalions shunned the clash, leaving the French Guards and the Scots Guards to their fate. Bonifaz and Bentivoglio's battalions pummelled the French Guard 'in revenge for Rocroi'.[109]

Châtillon realised the mistake of the *Gardes* leaving the centre of the line of battle so exposed, and filled the gap in his first line with the battalions of the second:[110] the regiments of Condé and Conti, with high morale, charged. Châtillon reorganised the *Gendamerie* squadrons into two large formations, took command of the first, with his aide Barbantane, lieutenant of the

---

104 Aumale, *Histoire des Princes de Condé*, p.251; Hardy, *Batailles Françaises*, p.116.
105 Godley, *The Great Condé*, p.225.
106 Aumale, *Histoire des Princes de Condé*, p.251. Hardy indicates that then there were 9 officers killed and 13 soldiers wounded. Hardy, *Batailles Françaises*, p.116.
107 Malo, *Champs de Bataille*, p.74.
108 Godley, *The Great Condé*, p.225; Thion, *Les Armées Françaises*, p.165.
109 Guthrie, *Batallas de la Guerra de los Treinta Años*, p.295.
110 Aumale, *Histoire des Princes de Condé*, p.251; Montglat highlights the Villette, Ravenel and Chappes regiments in this action. Montglat, *Collection des Mémoires*, p.100.

company d'Enghien, in charge of the second. Châtillon put spur to his horse and his men followed him, charging into the flank of the Spanish companies that were fighting in the gap left by the *Gardes*. The devastating charge of the two squadrons of *gendarmes* had its effect. The rest of the French infantry – Picardie, Persian, Condé, Conti, Mazarin regiments – also charged, encouraged by the example of the *Gendarmes*. The artillery was recovered, and the French second line was able to make contact with the *Gardes*, who were taking heavy casualties in the course of this aggressive action.[111]

Beck was fighting in the front line and a shot wounded him in the shoulder almost knocking him off his horse.[112] Officers, holding him on his horse despite his pain, tried to take him away from the battlefield, to save him from falling alive into the hands of the French,[113] however, he was captured by a lieutenant of Aumont's regiment. He would be taken to Arras in Condé's private carriage, where he would die of his wounds, refusing to accept the medical care which Condé offered out of consideration for his rank and accepted courage.[114] Beck died two days later without a word, tearing off his bandages to end a life he did not want to owe to the French:[115]

> [Beck] He only cursed during his imprisonment, not wanting to receive care from anyone, not even the Prince of Condé; so furious was he at the loss of this battle and at finding himself in the hands [now] of the one whom he believed he himself would capture.[116]

Faced with the attack of the French cavalry and infantry, the first line of Spanish infantry collapsed,[117] they became disorganised and began to flee, breaking through and disorganising the reserve units commanded by Fuensaldaña, who joined in the fighting too late:[118]

> The Catholic King's infantry is left alone. It made a vigorous effort, stopped for a moment the wheel of Fortune; now, enveloped on all sides, the army of France presses in on it. Discouragement has replaced overconfidence. Those Walloon, Italian, Lorrainer and Spanish battalions, so carefully interspersed, move away,

---

111 Hardy, *Batailles Françaises*, p.116; Malo, *Champs de Bataille*, p.74; Montglat, *Collection des Mémoires*, p.100.

112 Aumale claims that, according to a contemporary document, Beck was mortally wounded by the cavalry officer Robert de Gallery. Aumale, *Histoire des Princes de Condé*, p.256.

113 Aumale, *Histoire des Princes de Condé*, p.254; Malo, *Champs de Bataille*, p.75.

114 Godley, *The Great Condé*, p.225; Montglat, *Collection des Mémoires*, p.101; Thion, *Les Armées Françaises*, p.165.

115 Aumale, *Histoire des Princes de Condé*, p.256; Malo, *Champs de Bataille*, p.75.

116 Montglat, *Collection des Mémoires*, p.101.

117 In his brief account of the battle, the Conde de Fuensaldaña blames the defeat on the fact that Condé launched a counter-attack when the Spanish cavalry was manoeuvring to withdraw from the centre of the battlefield so that the infantry could take its place. This brief explanation is not consistent with the accounts in other contemporary sources or with the views of other historians. Pérez, 'Relación de lo Sucedido', p.550.

118 For Aumale and for Malo, the Spanish reserve units 'took too long because of Fuensaldaña's caution and the Archduke's hesitation, unable to mitigate this defeat and being swept away by the fugitives'. Aumale, *Histoire des Princes de Condé*, p.253; Malo, *Champs de Bataille*, p.73.

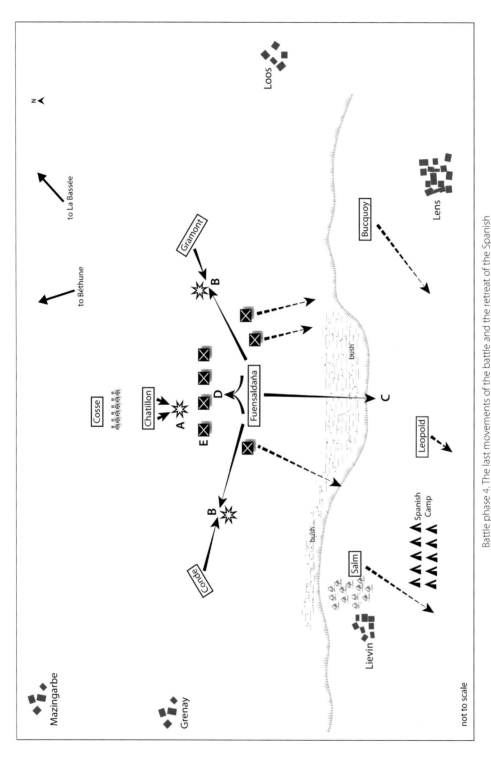

Battle phase 4. The last movements of the battle and the retreat of the Spanish

Faced with the attack of the French cavalry and infantry, the first line of Hispanic infantry collapsed (A), and they became disorganized and began to flee to Douai; breaking in and disorganizing the reserve squadrons commanded by Fuensaldaña, who joined the fight too late. Indeed, Spanish cavalry from Ligne and Fuensaldaña's corps was regrouping and trying to launch a counterattack (B), but they failed and they also withdraw from the battlefield (C). Ligne desperately reorganizes the infantry companies to defend the last line; he had thus managed to form a strong battalion, grouping companies from the center of the initial line of battle with various scattered units and his own units (E). Meanwhile, on the French side, the situation seemed to be under control. Having dispersed all the enemy cavalry (C), Condé and Gramont returned to the centre with their squadrons and halted in front of this cadre of Spanish infantry (D). The French attack and the Spanish infantrymen and those of other Nations request clemency, which is granted to them by Condé. The battle has been won by France.

come nearer, disperse, mix without recognising each other, and end by gathering in obedience to a kind of instinct and the force of tradition.[119]

Hardy has some words of praise for these soldiers:

> However, these Spanish, Italian and Walloon infantry are brave, many of whom were at Rocroi and remember it. They stop, assemble into a single battalion and fire their last charges of gunpowder.[120]

Indeed, the Prince de Ligne was regrouping as many men as he could, trying to reorganise the companies to defend the line, and he had thus succeeded in forming a strong battalion, grouping companies recovered from the centre with his own units.[121]

Meanwhile, on the French side the situation seemed to be under control. Having dispersed all the enemy cavalry, Condé and Gramont returned to the centre with their squadrons and halted in front of this cadre of Spanish infantry. The French horses, which had not eaten or drunk for 24 hours, seemed incapable of making a last great effort; the cavalrymen and infantrymen were also exhausted. But Condé knew that this was the decisive moment and he rose in his saddle so that his men could hear him: 'We have to finish off these invaders! Roche, Charge!'[122]

Roche was the lieutenant of his company of *Gardes*; only 18 of the 50 men of the company who had started the battle remained mounted. The survivors followed their commander's order and charged into the Spanish infantry body.[123] The Spanish infantry, formed in a large square, initially tried to resist. If at Rocroi the Spanish infantry presented a strong defence, made up of Spanish units, here at Lens the square surrendered since, according to the chronicler, these battalions were gathered from many nations, and no proud tradition held them together.[124]

In Hardy's words:

> The Spanish infantry no longer thought of fighting. Seeing themselves surrounded by our cavalry and attacked by Roche, they threw down their pikes and muskets, asking for quarter, hands together, knees on the ground.[125]

---

119 Malo, *Champs de Bataille*, p.75.
120 Hardy, *Batailles Françaises*, p.117.
121 Godley, *The Great Condé*, p.225.
122 Aumale, *Histoire des Princes de Condé*, p.254; Hardy, *Batailles Françaises*, p.117.
123 Hardy, *Batailles Françaises*, p.117; Malo, *Champs de Bataille*, p.75.
124 Godley, *The Great Condé*, p.225.
125 Hardy, *Batailles Françaises*, p.117.

The French conceded quarter. The battle was over, it had lasted less than three hours.[126] According to Hardy, 'but seldom has victory been more complete'.[127] The climactic part of the engagement had lasted just over an hour.[128]

Leopold had succumbed to pressure from the Spanish commanders and agreed to allow them to attack, and had then confessed and fled the battlefield seeing that the battle was lost, according to an eyewitness Jesuit priest, who was part of the Archduke's entourage.[129]

Archduke Leopold and the Conde de Fuensaldaña retreated to Douai with the remnants of their army.[130] The *lieutenants généraux* Erlach and La Ferté-Senneterre, with the *maréchaux de camp* Noirmoutier and Saint-Mégrin, had pushed the Spanish fugitives into the Lens Gorge; and later French scouts reported that the Spanish were marching towards Douai without stopping, without making any attempt to reorganise and present a new front.

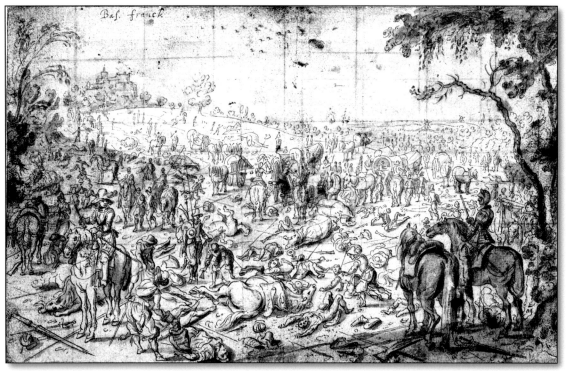

Pillaging the battlefield. Sebastian Vrancx, before 1647 (Rijksmuseum, Amsterdam)

126 Guthrie sets the timetable for the battle (Guthrie, *Batallas de la Guerra de los Treinta Años*, p.296):

    05:00 am The French retreat. First skirmishes.
    06:30 am The Archduke advances.
    08:00 am Armies fall into line of battle.
    08:30 am French cavalry attacks.
    09:00 am The battle begins in the centre.
    11:30 am The Spanish surrender.

127 Godley, *The Great Condé*, p.225.
128 Hardy, *Batailles Françaises*, p.117.
129 Godley, *The Great Condé*, p.225; Thion, *Les Armées Françaises*, p.165. This story of the explanation for the Spanish general's behaviour at Lens resembles the story about General Melo who, after the defeat at Rocroi, had also fled the battlefield, according to the French versions, although the Spanish versions say nothing about either Melo or Leopold.
130 Montglat, *Collection des Mémoires*, p.101.

Condé and Gramont met beyond the Lens ravine, and sword in hand, the Prince embraced the *Maréchal*. Gramont tells the anecdote that their two mounts became engaged in a fight, as if the horses were still upset by the combat they had experienced, 'and almost endangered the lives of their masters more than the battle itself'.[131]

Condé ordered his troops to advance towards Lens, which was defended by a garrison of about 600 men. They reached the fortress about noon, and had a great surprise in that the town had already surrendered. Villequier had been captured at the beginning of the battle and taken to the fortress; when the Spanish retreated towards Douai, Villequier had the nerve to speak to the officers of the garrison and frighten them by telling them that if they did not surrender, they would suffer reprisals from Condé, who would be enraged at losing time in capturing the fortress; if they surrendered immediately, this would please the Prince and he would spare their lives. So, when Condé arrived in front of the fortress, Villequier received Condé at the gates and presented him with the keys of the town. Villequier went from prisoner to conqueror in a matter of minutes.[132]

The Army of Flanders, according to the French, suffered 3,000 dead and 8,000 prisoners,[133] including 800 officers and non-commissioned officers, and *reformados*; 120 Standards and Colours were taken along with 38 cannon, the army's treasury, a large convoy of food and ammunition and all of the baggage. Of the prisoners, about 300 were native Spanish. 600 wounded were taken into Arras for treatment and some even went over to the French army.[134]

Montglat claims that:

> Never was a battle as fully won as that one, in which all the cannon and baggage were taken. The Standards and Colours were sent to the Queen, who had them hung in the church of Les Feuillans, because the Battle of Lens was won on Saint Bernard's Day, 19 August.[135]

Among the important prisoners captured by the French were, the Prince de Ligne, Conde de Saint-Amour, Marqués de Grana, Marqués de Saint-Martin,

---

131 Aumale, *Histoire des Princes de Condé*, p.253; Malo, *Champs de Bataille*, p.75; Thion, *Les Armées Françaises*, p.162.

132 Aumale, *Histoire des Princes de Condé*, p.251; Malo, *Champs de Bataille*, p.75.

133 All French sources agree over the number of Spanish dead. Aumale and Malo both affirm that the prisoners numbered 5,000. Aumale, *Histoire des Princes de Condé*, p.260; Hardy, *Batailles Françaises*, p.118; Malo, *Champs de Bataille*, p.76; Maffi, *En Defensa del Imperio*, 2014, p.108; Quincy, *Histoire Militaire*, p.98. Godley agrees on the number of Spanish dead, but indicates that the Army of Flanders had about 5,000 prisoners and wounded, Godley, *The Great Condé*, p.225; Wilson states that the Spanish dead numbered 3,000 and the prisoners 5,000, Wilson: *Europe's Tragedy*, p.507.

134 Janicki, 2009, p.2.

135 Montglat, *Collection des Mémoires*, p.101. The convent of the Bernardine monks, commonly called 'Couvent des Feuillants', although its official name was *Monastère Royal de Saint Bernard*, was located in rue Saint-Honoré, near the Tuileries Palace. The name 'feuillants' came from the Cistercian abbey of Notre-Dame de Feuillant in the former diocese of Rieux, near Toulouse in Haute-Garonne, the origin of this Bernardine congregation.

Baron de Crèvecoeur and *Maestres de Campo* Bernabé de Vargas, Fernando de Solis, Gabriel de Toledo, Hurtado de Mendoza, Miguel de Luna.[136]

According to the French,[137] the list of important prisoners included *Maestre de Campo General* Beck, *Teniente General* (Lieutenant General) Francisco Alberda, *Teniente General de Caballería* (Lieutenant General of cavalry) de Ligne,[138] *Intendente General* (Quartermaster General) Melchor de Luna, 7 *maestres de campo*, 8 colonels, a sergeant major, two quartermasters, four lieutenant colonels, 6 aides-de-camp, 196 captains,[139] 23 *reformado* captains, 95 lieutenants, 154 ensigns, 179 *reformado* ensigns, 106 sergeants, 61 *reformado* sergeants, and 8 officers of artillery.[140]

Because the number of prisoners was so great, and since it was necessary to send them to France with sufficient escort to lead them safely, Condé ordered Villequier to command two regiments of cavalry and one of infantry to escort them. As a result, the army was forced to remain close to the battlefield for eight days to await the return of the troops, who took the prisoners to Arras and La Bassée, which required several journeys.[141]

The French lost about 1,500 men, both killed and wounded.[142] The unit with the highest casualties was the *Gardes Françaises*; there was a high percentage of casualties among officers of cavalry and among officers of Condé's staff; but the casualties were also heavy in the squadrons of the *Gendarmerie*, and to a lesser degree, in the regiments of *Gardes Éscossaises*, *Gardes Suisses*, and the *Régiment de Picardie*. A full list of French casualties by regiment is given in Appendix II.[143]

According to Malo, Condé sent King Louis XIV a relation of the battle and in it he added: 'Remember the unfortunate *gendarmes*; they have earned what is owed to them.'[144]

The Prince of Condé was sad to learn of the death of the veteran Louis, Marquis de Normanville, and of the young brothers Louis and Francois de Champagne. As for La Moussaye, it was initially known only that he had

---

136 *Documents relatifs à la bataille de Lens*, pp.31–44: note the exhaustive list of prisoners; Aumale, *Histoire des Princes de Condé*, p.256; Hardy, Batailles Françaises, p.118; Montglat, *Collection des Mémoires*, p.101. See also Appendix IV.

137 *Documents relatifs à la bataille de Lens*, pp.31–44.

138 The Prince de Ligne spent almost three years in French prisons, until he was freed in exchange for a ransom of 80,000 florins. Fernando González de León, *The Road to Rocroi Class, Culture and Command in the Spanish Army of Flanders, 1567–1659*. (Leiden: Brill, 2009), p.213.

139 According to the Spanish ms 2379, copying a French source: 132 captains with command, 25 reformed captains, 100 lieutenants, 217 second lieutenants with command; 207 reformed second lieutenants, 91 sergeants with command and 65 reformed sergeants (BNH, Mss. 2379, 'Sucesos', f..201).

140 BNH, Mss. 2379, 'Sucesos', f.200. For a more detailed list see Appendix IV.

141 Thion, *Les Armées Françaises*, p.162.

142 Aumale, *Histoire des Princes de Condé*, p.260; Hardy, *Batailles Françaises*, p.118; Godley, *The Great Condé*, p.225; Wilson: *Europe's Tragedy*, p.507. In *Batailles*, he is informed of the French having 600 dead men. *Batailles*, 1696, p.212.

143 See also *Documents relatifs à la bataille de Lens*, pp.27–29.

144 Aumale, *Histoire des Princes de Condé*, p.260; Malo, *Champs de Bataille*, p.76. Condé was pleased to do justice to all those who had supported him well; thus, two months later, presenting the general Erlach to Louis XIV, he said to the King, 'Sire, here is the man to whom you owe the victory of Lens'. Aumale, *Histoire des Princes de Condé*, p.266; Malo, *Champs de Bataille*, p.76.

been wounded, although after a few days, it was learned that the Spaniards had taken him during their retreat to Douai, and he was a prisoner, alive if not well.[145]

That night Châtillon rode to Paris with Condé's report of the victory, a victory that would allow Mazarin to breathe easier. Godley states that for Mazarin, 'The defeat of the Spanish Army meant the peace of Europe,' the battle coinciding with the peace negotiations taking place in the cities of Osnabrück and Münster, the conclusion of which would become the Peace of Westphalia.[146]

According to Hardy, Lens was the most complete, the most irreparable defeat the Spanish had suffered since the beginning of the Thirty Years' War; and the battle essentially ended the war between France and Spain.[147] However, this statement does not correspond to reality, since the war between the two powers lasted until 1659, and the two armies enjoyed victories and suffered defeats in the following years: the war was not only fought in Flanders, but also in Catalonia, in Italy and in Germany.

With the news of the great victory in Flanders, Mazarin, who was always noted for his intelligence and diplomatic skill, knew that this was the moment he had to show his gratitude and magnanimity to Condé, who had once again given France a great victory. Indeed, the prince was hailed by the Court as their saviour. Gaston d'Orléans and his supporters 'disappeared' from the political scene and the palace intrigues, at least for a few days, also subsided; this was also a success for Mazarin.[148]

On 26 August 1648, after the singing of the *Te Deum* in Notre-Dame Cathedral for the victory of Lens, Mazarin had arrested three councillors of the Parliament, known to be his most poisonous opponents.[149] The Parisian people rose up in arms and within hours 200 barricades were erected throughout the city. The event became known as the *Journée des Barricades* (the Day of the Barricades)[150] and *Maréchal* La Meilleraye had great difficulty, with the few companies of *Gardes Françaises* and *Gardes Suisses* to hand, in restoring order and arresting the most dangerous troublemakers. Some Court personalities, terrified by these people, took refuge in Rueil.[151]

---

145 Godley, *The Great Condé*, p.226.

146 Godley, *The Great Condé*, p.226.

147 Hardy, *Batailles Françaises*, p.118.

148 Godley, *The Great Condé*, p.226.

149 Wilson: *Europe's Tragedy*, p.507.

150 The people of Paris, enraged by the arrest of Potier de Blancmesnil and Pierre Broussel, councillors to the Paris *Parlement*, gathered in various parts of the city, erecting more than 200 barricades. Louis Charton, who was also to be arrested, managed to escape. People shouted *Vive le Roi! Point de Mazarin!* ('Long live the King! Out with Mazarin!'). The next day, due to popular pressure, the two leaders were released. This incident is considered the beginning of the Fronde. Marc Hersant, 'La Journée des Barricades (27 août 1648)' in Jean Garapon, Jean i Zonza, et Christian (dir.): *Nouveaux Regards sud les Mémoires du Cardinal de Retz: actes du colloque organisé parell l'Université de Nantes*, Narr, coll. 'Biblio 17' N. 196, 2011, p.113–122.

151 Hardy, *Batailles Françaises*, p.118.

7

Repercussions

For Spain, Lens was a catastrophic defeat. In Brussels and Madrid it was feared that the French would launch a major offensive against Flanders and that that offensive could not be contained given the large number of casualties and prisoners from the defeat at Lens.[1]

The French headquarters remained at Lens for eight days, to allow the troops a well-deserved rest. In addition, the garrisons at Béthune and Arras were provisioned and strengthened.[2] Condé had been waiting for a letter from the Court explaining the riots in Paris and requesting his help, but he received only a letter from Minister Le Tellier with an order to send troops under Vidame to suppress the riots.[3]

Mazarin wrote a letter to his diplomats in Germany on 21 August, the same day that he learned the news of the Battle of Lens, to explain the victory over the Spanish Army, 'So that, in the present situation, which is the crisis of negotiation, you may be informed as soon as possible of such an important event which may have so many consequences in every way'.[4] The astute minister knew that this victory had to be publicised as a great success for the French armies in order to put pressure on the negotiations at Osnabrück and Münster.

Condé wanted to secure the maritime border of Flanders and so he planned to retake Furnes, and he sent a letter to Rantzau asking him about operational plans. The news that the French were planning to attack Furnes reached Sfondrato, who spread the word that he had a great many troops in Nieuwpoort to help Furnes, hearing this, Rantzau did not begin any movements. Fearing an invasion of maritime Flanders, the Archduke asked the towns for soldiers and money.[5]

Condé did not want to waste time, and he sent reinforcements and urged Rantzau to surround Furnes: this small town was important because it

---

1   BNH, Mss. 2379, 'Sucesos', f.80.
2   Aumale, *Histoire des Princes de Condé*, p.268.
3   Aumale, *Histoire des Princes de Condé*, p.269.
4   Jules Mazarin, *Lettres du Cardinal Mazarin Pendant son Ministère*, tome 3 (Paris: Imprimerie Nationale, 1883), p.181.
5   Aumale, *Histoire des Princes de Condé*, p.269.

Commemorative medal of the Battle of Lens, minted in 1648. The obverse shows the head of King Louis XIV. The legend on the coin is in Latin: *LUDOVICUS XIIII REX CHRISTIANISS* [The Most Christian King Louis XIV]. The reverse shows the image of a goddess (Athene?) symbolising France, leaning on her shield and holding a long spear, trampling a defeated Spanish soldier; behind her, are trophies of arms with the banner of Castile and the legend: *LEGIONVM HISPAN. RELIQVIAE DELETAE* (The last Spanish legions destroyed). (Stephen Ede-Borrett collection)

threatened Dunkirk. Rantzau, accompanied by Vaubecour and Castelnau, marched on the town with 5,000 troops.[6] As they approached Furnes, Rantzau encountered an entrenched post defended by the troops of the Marqués Sfrondrato, strategically placed in such a way as to prevent the French from laying siege to Furnes. Rantzau used his artillery to cover the frontal assault of his troops, and in a fight that lasted two hours, forced Sfondrato's retreat towards Nieuwpoort. Rantzau opened the siege of Furnes on 27 August and began to bombard it with his artillery.[7]

On 29 August Mazarin sent Condé a letter in which he explained his version of the revolts of the *Journée des Barricades*, stating that 'everything is now as calm as if nothing had happened,' and authorised Condé to manoeuvre his army, 'as you see fit, without the affairs of the country imposing any restrictions on you.'[8]

The siege of Furnes was not progressing in the way that it should have. In the letters that Rantzau sent to Condé, the latter continually read about difficulties, unforeseen events, excuses... The Prince decided to take charge of the siege personally.[9]

On 7 September the Prince of Condé arrived at Furnes – because of a slight illness, he had to travel by sloop through the canals to the coast at Furnes[10] – and with his energetic determination the siege intensified. Condé wished to finish the siege as soon as possible, so he wanted to set an example

6   Montglat, *Collection des Mémoires*, p.101.
7   Aumale, *Histoire des Princes de Condé*, p.272; Montglat, *Collection des Mémoires*, p.102.
8   Aumale, *Histoire des Princes de Condé*, p.270.
9   Aumale, *Histoire des Princes de Condé*, p.273.
10   Aumale, *Histoire des Princes de Condé*, p.270–274.

to his men by moving up to the front line, but exposed in a trench, he was wounded in the hip by a musket shot.[11]

On 8 September the counterscarp was reached, and the defenders, seeing that soon the walls of the town would be assaulted, asked for clemency and on 10 September, seeing that there was no hope of relief, they surrendered.[12] The infantry garrison, the regiments of Ritbergh and Ottavio Guasco and some independent Walloon companies, were to be exchanged for the prisoners taken in the attempted taking of Ostend. News of the town's capture was carried to the Court by *Maréchal de Bataille* de Fors.[13]

After the capture of Furnes, the Prince de Condé would have liked to have continued his advance into the interior of Flanders, but the Queen requested his presence at Court on the grounds that he had to recover from his wound[14] and forbade him to take any further action because of the open conflict with the nobility and the people in the streets of Paris. Montglat writes that these disturbances, 'almost put an end to France's prosperity and were thought to be throwing it over the precipice, from which France will emerge in the end more glorious than ever'.[15]

The Archduke took advantage of this respite and gathered the survivors of Lens, together with new troops recruited in Germany and by Flanders, and formed a new army. When the French took Furnes, the Archduke already had troops mustered to defend the territory.[16]

On 28 August, Archduke Leopold Wilhelm wrote to King Philip IV to give his version of the battle. The Archduke barely mentions the Lorrainer cavalry – probably resentful of their delay in joining the campaign at the beginning of the summer – despite their prominent role in the first phase of the fighting. He does not mention Ligniville either, but he does mention Beck, whom he praises for his courage and regrets his loss. The Archduke severely judges the *compagnies franches*, whom he considered unprepared, but he praises the courage of the foot soldiers, and especially of the Spanish tercios and he singles out the tercios of the Marqués de Bonifaz and the Marqués de Bentivoglio, to whom he attributes the honour of having defeated the French *Garde*.[17]

The defeat at Lens led to a restructuring of the Spanish chain of command in Flanders: the rank of *Sargento General de Batalla de Caballería* (Sergeant General of Battle of the Cavalry) was created, a rank which had first been used in the Army of Alsace – a Spanish Army created in 1633 for the campaign in Alsace of 1633–1634 conducted by the Duque de Feria and the *Cardinal-Infante*. This new post was to replace the *Comisario General de la Caballería* (Commissary General of the Cavalry), which had been useless in the effort to order and control the various cavalry units of the Spanish Army in Flanders. The position of *Sargento General de Batalla de Caballería* had the

11 Aumale, *Histoire des Princes de Condé*, p.274.
12 Montglat, *Collection des Mémoires*, p.102; Quincy, *Histoire Militaire*, p.98.
13 Aumale, *Histoire des Princes de Condé*, p.276.
14 Aumale, *Histoire des Princes de Condé*, p.276.
15 Montglat, *Collection des Mémoires*, p.102.
16 Pérez, 'Relación de lo Sucedido', p.551; BNH, Mss. 2379, 'Sucesos', f.80.
17 Aumale, *Histoire des Princes de Condé*, p.258.

same functions as the equivalent in the Imperial and French armies – to coordinate the cavalry units in war and to look after their organisation and operational status in peacetime.[18]

After the defeat of Lens, the Council of State in Madrid ordered that all the cavalry companies of all nations serving in the Spanish Army be merged into larger units, called either cavalry tercios or cavalry regiments;[19] the rank of *Maestres de Campo de Caballería* was created for the former, and *Coronel de Caballería* (Colonel of Cavalry) for the latter. Both commands were, of course, subordinate to, and answerable to, the *Sargento General de Batalla de Caballería*.[20]

Spanish cavalry during the siege of La Bassée in 1642. Petrus Rucholle, 1642 (Rijksmuseum, Amsterdam)

1648 was the year of the consolidation of the victory of France and Sweden. The allied armies of Königsmark, Turenne and Wrangel were advancing towards Vienna and Prague. Bavaria and Austria were on the verge of collapse, and the Protestant States were on the verge of total victory. From Rome, Pope Innocent X tried to mediate between the fighting nations, attempting to favour the Catholics but, unsurprisingly, the Protestants refused, however, the Republic of Venice offered mediation, which was accepted by all sides. The Catholic diplomats were in Münster and the Protestants in Osnabrück.[21]

Each of the contenders on the battlefield also sought to achieve some success in diplomatic negotiations, which is why the negotiations were so difficult. The Emperor Ferdinand III and the elderly Elector Maximilian I of Bavaria, in 1648 he was 75, had to accept the peace terms of their enemies – in Münster with France and in Osnabrück with Sweden. The first negotiations had begun as early as 1644, at the height of the war, but the vicissitudes of war meant that the belligerent parties were more or less interested in signing the peace depending on the results in the battlefield. The final agreement, known as the Peace of Westphalia, was signed on 24 October 1648, formally ending the Thirty Years' War.[22]

For France, in its war against The Empire, it was resolved that the Bishoprics of Metz, Toul, and Verdun should re-join France and be separated

---

18   González de León, *The Road to Rocroi*, p.26; Maffi, *En Defensa del Imperio*, p.332.
19   Maffi, *En Defensa del Imperio*, pp.204–210.
20   González, 2009, p.26. The Archduke wrote to King Philip IV complaining about the performance of the cavalry and especially of the officers, complaining that many of them had been promoted simply because they were members of the nobility. González de León, *The Road to Rocroi*, pp.338–339, 353, 368; Maffi, *En Defensa del Imperio*, pp.410–413.
21   Montglat, *Collection des Mémoires*, p.93.
22   Wilson: *Europe's Tragedy*, pp.514–533.

from The Empire; that Upper and Lower Alsace, and the town of Breisach (situated on the right bank of the Rhine) and the counties of Béfort and Ferette, should also be ceded to the French. France was also to have a garrison at Philippsburg, on the far side of the Rhine, albeit that the city remained the property of the Elector of Trier. France also wanted an agreement that The Emperor could not directly or indirectly aid the King of Spain, even in Franche-Comté, although that was within an Imperial *Kreis* (Circle), nor would The Empire interfere in support of the Duc de Lorraine.[23]

France gained a presence and a vote at the Imperial Diet, and with its new possessions on the Rhine it achieved the long-cherished dream of interrupting the 'Spanish Road' (*Camino Español*) that had connected the Spanish possessions in Italy with its dominions and allies in Flanders and The Empire. Mazarin, for his part, ensured Ferdinand III's neutrality in the Spanish-French conflict, a term that led to Spain's refusal to sign the treaty.[24]

For Sweden, The Empire was to pay a war indemnity of five million thalers; in addition, the peace treaty granted it Western Pomerania, the cities of Stettin and Wismar, the islands of Rugen, Usedom and Wollin, and the secularised Bishoprics of Verden and Bremen. Sweden was now undisputedly the master of the Baltic, it had control of the Weser, Elbe and Oder estuaries. Sweden also now had a territorial empire in Germany, as Gustav II Adolf had dreamed of, and the King of Sweden became an Imperial prince, entitled to a seat in the Imperial Diet, additionally the country had the right to send deputies to the Imperial Diet, and to have a deliberative voice there.[25]

Frederick William, Elector of Brandenburg, became one of the most influential German Protestant leaders thanks to the Peace. He was granted the adjacent territories of Halberstadt and Minden, and Eastern Pomerania. By the Treaty of Stettin of 1653 he gained Central Pomerania.

Saxony saw its possession of Lusatia recognised; and the Herzog von Württemberg, the Landgraf von Hesse-Cassel and the Markgraf von Baden-Durlach, who had lost their territories at the Peace of Prague (1635), were restored to their former domains.[26]

As for the Electorate of the Palatinate (*Kurpfalz*), associated with the region of the Upper Palatinate (*Oberpfalz*), it was agreed that the Duke of Bavaria should be its elector, but that an eighth electorate would be created in the Lower Palatinate – also called the Rhine Palatinate (*Rheinpfalz*) – to be held by Charles I Louis, the eldest son of the late Elector Palatine Frederick V, the 'Winter King' of Bohemia, for him and his male heirs of the Wittelsbach-Simmern family. It was set out that if the direct male blood line died out, that electorate would be abolished. Something similar would happen if the male line of the Duke of Bavaria from the Wittelsbach family died out in which case the original Electorate Palatine would revert to the family branch of Frederick V, and the eighth electorate would be abolished.[27]

---

23   Montglat, *Collection des Mémoires*, p.94.
24   Galán, *La Paz de Westfalia* p.22.
25   Galán, *La Paz de Westfalia* p.23; Montglat, *Collection des Mémoires*, p.94.
26   Galán, *La Paz de Westfalia* p.23; Montglat, *Collection des Mémoires*, p.94.
27   Montglat, *Collection des Mémoires*, p.94.

But France and Spain did not make peace – the war that had begun in 1635 was not over a religious issue but over world hegemony. Thus, the Franco-Spanish war continued for 11 more years, ending officially on 7 November 1659, with the signing of the Treaty of the Pyrenees on the Isle of Pheasants (on the Bidasoa River, on the Franco-Spanish border), by Luis Méndez de Haro and Pedro Coloma, on behalf of Philip IV of Spain, and Cardinal Mazarin and Hugues de Lionne, on behalf of Louis XIV.

However, the French victory was not as swift as modern historians of the seventeenth century military Revolution have made it out to be, describing the Spanish military model as archaic and the French as superior. Had this truly been the case, it would not have taken France 25 years to defeat Spain.

Despite the defeat at Lens in August 1648, and the signing of the Peace between France and The Empire in which The Emperor Ferdinand III undertook not to aid his cousin Philip IV, and the peninsular wars against Portugal and Catalonia, the army of the Spanish Monarchy was still a force to be reckoned with.

Additionally, the internal conflict of the Fronde broke out in France, which ravaged the country for five years (1648–1653);[28] the discontent of the population, the nobility and the French institutions with the cost of the war and the resultant high tax burden, was exacerbated by a rise in prices and an increase in royal power. All of which led to armed uprisings throughout the country.

The Regent of France, Anne of Austria (1601–1666), engraving by Robert Nanteuil created *c.* 1661. In accordance with the marriage agreement signed in 1611 Anne was married in Burgos, by proxy, to Louis XIII of France (1601–1643) on 18 October 1615. On the same day, in Bordeaux, Princess Isabel de Bourbon, sister of Louis XIII, married Prince Philip, the future Philip IV of Spain, again by proxy. Both princesses quickly travelled to their new countries. Anne always behaved like a 'native' Frenchwoman, defending the rights of her husband and later, as Regent, of her son Louis XIV. (Metropolitan Museum of Art, New York)

---

28 The existing bibliography, in both French and English, about the conflict of the Fronde is abundant. In English: R. Bonney, *Society and Government in France under Richelieu and Mazarin, 1624–1661*, (Leicester: University of Leicester Press, 1988); G. S. Gordon, *The Fronde*, (Oxford: B. H. Blackwell, 1905; P. Knachel, *England and the Fronde. The Impact of the English Civil War and Revolution on France* (New York: Ithaca, 1967); L. Moote, *The Revolt of the Judges: The Parlement of Paris and the Fronde, 1643–1652* (Princeton: Princeton University Press, 1971); D. Parrot, *1652. The Cardinal, The Prince, and the Crises of the 'Fronde'*, (Oxford: OUP, 2020); P. Sonnino, *Mazarin's Quest: The Congress of Westphalia and the Coming of the Fronde* (Harvard: Harvard University Press, 2008. In French: J. M. Constant, *C'Était la Fronde* (Paris: Flammarion, 2016); R. Duchêne & P. Ronzeaud, (eds.), *La Fronde en Questions* (Aix-en-Provence, Universtié de Provence, 1989); E. H. Kossmann, *La Fronde* (Leiden: Universitaire Pers Leiden, 1954); L. Madelin, *La Fronde* (Paris: Plon, 1931); H. Méthivier, *La Fronde* (Paris, PUF, 1984); M. Pernot, *La Fronde* (Paris, Éditions de Fallois, 1994); O. Ranum, *La Fronde*, (Paris, Éditions du Seuil, 1995). In France, the decade of 1950 started a boom about studies of the Fronde, these studies are especially intense on the part of both Marxist historians and their detractors.

The riots in Paris in January and August 1648 began the period known as the *Fronde des Parlementaires* (1648–1649): a rebellion initiated by the Paris *Parlement* against Mazarin's economic measures. The Queen and the Cardinal had to give in, appeasing the masses, but without resolving the problem.

The outbreak of the conflict of the Fronde meant for the Spanish Court a respite in the war against France. Just as the French Wars of Religion of the sixteenth century had taken the country out of pan European affairs for several decades, the political conflict between Louis XIV, the Regent Anne of Austria and her minister Mazarin against much of the great French nobility would mean a setback for the French armies on all fronts and the collapse of their chain of command.

This internal conflict was exploited by Spain. Since 1648, with the Treaty of Westphalia, France had been left alone in the conflict: its German and Swedish allies were satisfied with the peace agreements, and The United Provinces had achieved *de jure* independence recognised by Spain, so they no longer continued their war. Spain now had Flanders free of the constant threat of war on two fronts, so it could focus on offensive operations against French frontier towns. And as for the French southern frontier, the Spanish were aware of the discontent of the Catalan civilian population against the French authorities, who oppressed with heavy taxation those that they had come to 'liberate' in 1641!

Expectations for the 1649 campaign in Flanders were high in both Madrid and Brussels.[29] The Archduke was aware of the intrigues of the Paris *Parlement* against the Regent and the Cardinal, and messages were exchanged; a first Frondist plan proposed that Fuensaldaña should move ahead of a detachment of 4,000 horsemen and 1,000 dragoons, and harass the countryside near Paris, awaiting a call from the Paris *Parlement* to support their insurrection. It was planned that two armies, under the orders of the Archduke and of the Duc de Lorraine, would also invade France to create a broad front. However, the plan did not materialise mainly because of the lack of help from the Frondists themselves.[30]

The Archduke was not resigned to doing nothing, so, with his staff, he planned that the objective of the 1649 campaign would be the taking of Ypres. In March, the Marqués Sfondrato, with half the army, blockaded Ypres, while the other half, commanded by Fuensaldaña, was to occupy Saint-Venant first, and thus secure that town before continuing on to the siege of Ypres. Saint-Venant surrendered after eight days. The Spanish Army reassembled in front of Ypres and after 20 days the town surrendered as well, allowing 400 French cavalry and 3,000 French infantry to march out and to return to France.[31]

The Spanish Army returned to Flanders, exhausted from the Lens campaign and the siege of Ypres. Between April and June there was no fighting, but on 19 June a French Army under Henri de Lorraine-Harcourt

---

29   Maffi, *En Defensa del Imperio*, p.112.
30   Maffi, *En Defensa del Imperio*, pp.112–113; Pérez, 'Relación de lo Sucedido', p.551.
31   Maffi, *En Defensa del Imperio*, p.113; Pérez, 'Relación de lo Sucedido', pp.551–552.

appeared in front of Cambrai, which was defended by the Conde de Garcies; on 2 July a reinforcement of three Walloon tercios was able to enter the city before the French completed the blockade of the town.[32]

The Spanish Army was assembled at Valenciannes and the Archduke asked the Duc de Lorraine for his troops, but Charles repeatedly made excuses and did not send them. After eight days of waiting for the Army of Lorraine, the Archduke ordered an advance. He passed Buchain and Arleux, approached Cambrai, and the army fortified itself at a point where the River Scheldt protected their left flank. An assault on the French line was prepared to introduce into the town a reinforcement of 1,500 infantry and several hundred cavalry: while a third of the army was left protecting the camp, another third, under Fuensaldaña, and the last third under Baron de Clichan would attack the French, creating a diversion and allowing the 1,500 infantry to get through. A thick fog covered the relief force but when the other two attacked, the relief troops were able to enter without difficulty. When the sun came up, the French saw more soldiers on the ramparts and noted the arrival of the reinforcements, so they decided to withdraw and fortify the village of Condé – they were closely followed by the Archduke. However, after a few days in Condé and feeling surrounded, the French withdrew, ending the campaign. Sfondrato took La Motte-au-Bois on 9 October, and the Army of Flanders then retreated into winter quarters.[33]

After months of intrigue and growing tension between Mazarin and the nobility[34] -*Parlement* declared Mazarin outlawed on 8 January 1649 – the Cardinal attempted to resolve the conflict by a bold authoritarian coup: on 18 January 1650 he ordered the arrest of the Prince de Condé, his brother the Prince de Conti, and the Governor of Normandy, Henri, Duc de Longueville; the three captured princes were imprisoned in Le Havre. The high nobility felt threatened by such an action and the situation did not improve.[35]

After the signing of peace with Spain, the Dutch authorities focused on rebuilding the country and the economy. However, the new *Stadtholder*, William II of Orange, planned to increase military spending and to continue the war with Spain, even though the Assemblies of the States of the Provinces were against it. William had opposed the Peace of Westphalia, and had since held secret negotiations with Mazarin to gain French support for a regime of centralised power in his person and to resume the war with Spain.[36]

In January 1650 the troops of the Duc de Lorraine, who had served for years with the Spanish armies, entered The United Provinces and sacked several towns. William II capitalised on this incident to pursue his aggressive military policy. He had succeeded in persuading the States General to give him dictatorial authority by a narrow margin of four votes to three. However, his actions to maintain a strong army, on which he would base his power,

32   Maffi, *En Defensa del Imperio*, p.113; Pérez, 'Relación de lo Sucedido', pp.553–554.
33   Maffi, *En Defensa del Imperio*, p.114; Pérez, 'Relación de lo Sucedido', pp.554–555.
34   Wilson: *Europe's Tragedy*, p.507.
35   J. Israel, 'España y Europa. Desde el Tratado de Münster a la Paz de los Pirineos, 1648–1659' in *Pedralbes*, 29 (2009), p.288.
36   Israel, 'España y Europa', p.288.

This painting depicts the interior of the Ridderzaal (Hall of Knights), one of the main rooms of the architectural complex of the Binnenhof in The Hague, during the Great Assembly of the States General in 1651; the work is attributed to Bartholomeus van Bassen. The Binnenhof is a complex of buildings located in the city centre of The Hague, which housed the seat of the States General of The Netherlands. After the death of the *stadholder* William II of Orange-Nassau in 1650 (a nephew of the great Maurice of Nassau), the States General held a special general assembly to decide whether it was convenient to renew that political-military rank of *stadholder*. In the assembly, the representatives of The United Provinces decided not to appoint a new *stadholder*. Van Bassen's painting shows the large number of Standards and Colours hanging from the ceiling and the walls belonging to the Spanish armies, which were trophies of battle.[37] A large number of the flags were captured by Maurice of Nassau in the Battles of Turnhout in 1597 and Nieuwpoort in 1600. The flags with the coat of arms of Spain are Colours from tercios, while most of the flags with a white background are from other Infantry companies. In the background there are company flags, but with a blue background and cavalry standards. At the left is a flag with an armour arm with the hand holding a sword, possibly from a German regiment in the service of Spain, since this iconography is not common in the Spanish, Italian or Flemish Tercios. (Rijksmuseum, SK-C-1350)

---

37   The Dutch Army Museum still holds the remains of some of these Colours, although today they are in a very fragile and fragmentary condition. (ed.)

clashed with the more mercantilist views of the Province of Holland, led by the Regents of Amsterdam, Andries Bicker and Cornelis de Graeff, who called for a reduction of the army in accordance with the terms of the Peace of Münster, a call which William refused to accede to. He wanted to settle the conflict quickly, and on 30 July he imprisoned the six members of the Dutch Provincial Assembly who opposed him most, as well as Jacob de Witt, along with the mayors of Haarlem, Delft, Hoorn and Medemblik. They

The Spanish Army marching from Maastricht, 1632. Jan van de Velde (II), 1632. (Rijksmuseum, Amsterdam)

were imprisoned in Loevestein Castle and William sent his cousin Willem Frederic van Nassau-Dietz at the head of an army of 10,000 men to take Amsterdam by force, although bad weather prevented the campaign. With this power in his hands, William signed an alliance with France and England to resume the war with Spain, but his death from smallpox in November 1650 caused William's opponents to gain influence in the Assemblies of the States, with the result that they did not name any new *Stadtholder* for the Provinces of Holland, Zealand and Utrecht until 1672 and for Gelderland and Overijssel until 1675; the peace with Spain held.

All these events were followed with great concern in Flanders, where spies reported to Archduke Leopold Wilhelm on the growing power of William of Orange. The Conde de Fuensaldaña advised Leopold Wilhelm to launch an action against France, to take advantage of the fact that the political turmoil between the leader and the States in The Netherlands did not yet have a clear winner. Initially the plan was to attack Dunkirk, and the Governor of Nieuwpoort, Antonio Pimentel, took charge of collecting together the necessary supplies and siege equipment. On 12 February Fuensaldaña left Brussels with the mission of taking Dunkirk; however, not all of the troops that had been mobilised could arrive in time, so the attack could not be carried out.[38]

Over the next two months, the Archduke ordered the recruitment of infantry, amalgamated units into full regiments, and diplomats were sent to recruit cavalry regiments from Germany and from units discharged by The Empire. In addition, the Duc de Lorraine sent Baron de Clinchamp, at the head of an army of 4,000 men to participate in the campaign in Flanders.[39]

---

38 Juan Antonio Vincart, 'Relación de la Campaña de 1650' in *Colección de Documentos Inéditos para la Historia de España* (CODOIN), tome 75 (Madrid: Miguel Ginesta, 1880), pp.488–489.

39 Vincart, 'Relación de la Campaña', p.491.

When the Spanish Court learned of the outbreak of the Fronde, the imprisonment of Condé, Conti and Longueville,[40] and the disaffection of Turenne and other great nobles, the Archduke sent messengers to negotiate with the rebels, to find out how many men they could count on and to offer an alliance.[41]

Both in Madrid and Brussels two alternatives were considered: either to try to recover a major city from French hands, or to invade France to support the Fronde and try to take a city, and force the enemy to defend their land and territory. Those in favour of the first option argued that it was a tremendous risk to go deep into enemy territory, and that the success of the previous campaign should not be tempted; however at Turenne's insistence it was agreed that the second option would be the one to be pursued.[42]

The Army of Flanders launched an offensive south of Valenciennes, along the Oise valley, supported by a force led by *Maréchal* de Turenne, who was now one of the main leaders of the Fronde and had allied with the Spanish. Mouson was taken on 29 May, Hirson on 30 May, and on 3 June Turenne's army joined the Spanish Army at Neuve-Maison, marching the next day to Étréaupont after taking Le Câtelet.[43] On 5 June, the Spanish Army arrived in front of Guise, taking advantage of the situation to seize the surrounding towns. On 16 June, the entire Spanish Army was again concentrated – together with the Lorrainer and Fronde troops – to besiege Guise; on 21 June, all the siege work was completed and the bombardment began on the 26th.[44]

After some days, a force of 200 Italians, 100 Spaniards and 100 Germans, under the command of the Marqués de Bentivoglio, seized one of the city gates and forced the garrison to retreat to the citadel. The construction of a mine was begun although Turenne was wounded in the arm by a musket shot while inspecting the works. A force of 1,500 infantry was assembled for the assault on the citadel, but the mine, laid in the rock at the base of the citadel, failed to take effect in the wall.[45]

When a French relief army of about 13,000 men arrived at the end of June, it was decided to continue the siege, but the French sent a detachment of 1,000 cavalry and 1,000 infantry to attack the Spanish supply convoys coming from Avesnes, and managed to destroy a large supply convoy.[46] The Spanish decided to start the withdrawal towards La Capelle; they were continually harassed by the French army, but there was no formal battle. The Spanish were able to claim a small victory when the Croatian cavalry regiment captured a French supply convoy, taking 100 waggons and 260 prisoners.[47]

---

40   Modesto Lafuente, *Historia General de España,* tome XII (Barcelona: Montaner y Simón, 1889), p.44.
41   Pérez, 'Relación de lo Sucedido', p.555; Vincart, 'Relación de la Campaña', p.492.
42   Maffi, *En Defensa del Imperio*, p.116; Vincart, 'Relación de la Campaña', p.495.
43   Maffi, *En Defensa del Imperio*, p.117; Pérez, 'Relación de lo Sucedido', p.551; Vincart, 'Relación de la Campaña', p.501.
44   Vincart, 'Relación de la Campaña', pp.503–505.
45   Maffi, *En Defensa del Imperio*, p.117; Vincart, 'Relación de la Campaña', pp.505–507.
46   Maffi, *En Defensa del Imperio*, p.117.
47   Vincart, 'Relación de la Campaña', pp.509–510.

Interrupting the course of their movement, the Spanish besieged La Capelle on 23 July. After a week they managed to reach the counterscarp, which was taken the same day, along with the rest of the outer defensive positions. The Spanish then began to construct mines and to drain the ditch, at which point the defenders asked for terms of a surrender, which was formalised on 2 August.[48]

Although it was summer, during the sieges of Guise and La Capelle it had rained heavily, delaying the Spanish movements. Despite this, it was decided to continue to press the frontier. At this point a *muestra general* (general muster) was held and the Spanish Army mustered 13,000 cavalry and 16,000 infantry. On 3 August, the Marqués Sfondrato, at the head of 4,000 men, took Étréaupont, which he quickly fortified, since it represented a strategic bridge on the River Oise.[49]

A detachment under Fuensaldaña took Vervins without resistance. The main body of the Spanish Army continued to advance: from Vervins the army passed through La Neuville-Bosmont to Agnicourt-et-Séchelles and from there, on 13 August, they moved to besiege Marle, which surrendered without a fight, and the next day they took Montcornet. On the 15th they marched towards Renneville and, forewarned of the proximity of the French army, the Spanish troops marched in battle formation, as the meadows allowed such a deployment. Rethel surrendered without a fight on 17 August.[50]

While the Spanish Army was concentrated at Inaumont, the Conde de Fuensaldaña and *Maréchal* Turenne rode to the Château de Thugny, where Claude Lamoral I de Ligne, Prince de Ligne, was confined after his capture at the Battle of Lens: on his word of honour to the King of France, Ligne pledged not to escape, and he chose to be confined at Thugny, the property of his uncle.[51]

The French army, around 11,000 strong, was divided into 3 corps to cover more territory and to monitor Spanish movements. On 23 August, the

---

48   Vincart, 'Relación de la Campaña', pp.510–517.
49   Vincart, 'Relación de la Campaña', p.518.
50   Vincart, 'Relación de la Campaña', pp.518–519.
51   Vincart, 'Relación de la Campaña', p.520.

Archduke moved his army towards Neufchâtel-sur-Aisne, which fell on the 24th.[52]

Turenne advanced with his troops and part of the Lorrainer cavalry to the village of Fismes, where they discovered the army of *Maréchal* Charles de Monchy, Marquis de Hocquincourt, of about 4,000 troops was nearby. The two armies engaged in some fighting for the bridges over the River Vesle. During the fighting the *Maréchal* was twice captured by the Spanish and was twice rescued by his men. Finally, the French had to retreat, leaving behind 400 dead and 300 prisoners. Fismes was also taken by the Spanish.[53]

There was panic in Paris, and Mazarin did not know whether the Spaniards intended to march on Paris or to push further into other regions. The Archduke, who had taken up residence in the town of Bazoches, near Reims, sent the Duc d'Orléans a peace proposal, which was to be rejected.[54] However, the advances of the French Royalist troops forced the Archduke to retreat to the area of the River Meuse, attacking several towns in the Charleville-Mézières area and taking the town of Mouzon after a long siege during September and October.[55]

While all attention was focused on that frontier, a Spanish force of 300 cavalry and 500 infantry entered French territory from Saint-Omer and, from the vicinity of Abbeville, plundered 3,000 sheep, 600 cows and 100 horses, and captured 80 soldiers.[56]

However, news from The United Provinces reported that the Spanish advances had aroused fears among the Dutch authorities and that there was also a risk of clashes between the supporters of the States General and the supporters of *Stadtholder* William. Members of the Council of State, following a meeting on 16 August 1650, warned Philip IV that they felt that it was appropriate to halt the French campaign and await developments. In a secret letter sent to the Archduke, they also informed him that he should stop the offensive, and if the Province of Holland was attacked by the *Stadtholder*, the Army of Flanders should come to the aid of Holland and the other Provinces against the *Stadtholder*. In addition, in order not to give William an excuse to resume the war with Spain, Spanish diplomacy offered the States General a series of trade concessions and hinted at aid to the Dutch in their war against the Portuguese, who were conquering Dutch Brazil.[57]

The *Stadtholder* understood the Spanish diplomatic moves as a subtle aggressive manoeuvre against his centralising policy and, under Mazarin's auspices, offered to mediate between France and Spain to help find a negotiated solution to the war; such a proposal, far from being altruistic, concealed the threat that, if Dutch mediation was not accepted, the Provinces would back France again and break off relations. Madrid warned

---

52   Vincart, 'Relación de la Campaña', p.520.
53   Lonchay, *La Rivalité de la France*, p.154; Maffi, *En Defensa del Imperio*, p.117; Vincart, 'Relación de la Campaña', p.520.
54   Lonchay, *La Rivalité de la France*, p.154.
55   Lonchay, *La Rivalité de la France*, p.158; Pérez, 'Relación de lo Sucedido', p.558; Vincart, 'Relación de la Campaña', pp.528–536.
56   Vincart, 'Relación de la Campaña', p.536.
57   Israel, 'España y Europa', p.291.

the Archduke of this Dutch pressure and that he should act with the utmost caution, taking the Dutch proposals as a stratagem devised in collusion with Mazarin, and therefore delay his response as long as possible. Finally, the Archduke sent word to William that the Spanish were willing to negotiate peace with France, but neither accepting nor rejecting the Dutch mediation. This deliberate ambiguity angered the *Stadtholder*, but his death in 1650 ended the internal and external crisis of the fledgling Dutch Republic.[58]

Meanwhile, on 9 December 1650 in France, a powerful French army of more than 30,000 men had laid siege to Rethel, with the intention not only of recovering the important town, but more especially to boost the morale of the troops and the whole country and to restore the prestige of the Regent and the Cardinal. The siegeworks were commenced and a breach was quickly made in the walls: four assaults were made to storm the town, but they were all repulsed. Finally, faced with the impossibility of receiving reinforcements or relief, the garrison surrendered on 13 December, and 300 cavalry and 900 infantry left for Avesnes.[59]

In an attempt to relieve Rethel, Turenne assembled a force of 8,000 troops but arrived near Rethel two days after it had surrendered. The surrender was not known to Turenne and he ordered 3 cannon to be fired – the agreed signal and the agreement was that the garrison should reply with 3 more cannon; as nothing was heard the signal was repeated.

On seeing that Rethel had indeed surrendered, Turenne ordered his men to rest. It was then that the French Royal army appeared, and the Vicomte ordered his troops into their battle lines. On 15 December, around 7,000 French cavalry and 4,000 French infantry, under the command of César de Choiseul du Plessis-Praslin, faced off against some 6,000 French Frondist and Lorrainer cavalry and 3,000 French infantry. The battle initially went Turenne's way, but he was eventually defeated, losing about 2,000 men with a further 3,000 taken prisoner, while the Royalists suffered around 1,000 casualties.[60]

Engraving of a musketeer with an older style musket with a rest. Salomon Savery, between 1635 and 1655 (Stephen Ede-Borrett collection)

In the other theatres of the war with France, in the regions of Italy and Catalonia, Philip IV's arms were successful. In Italy, Juan José of Austria launched a campaign against the French held towns of Piombino and Porto Longone. On 11 May 1650 he sailed from Naples at the head of a fleet of 30 Neapolitan and Sicilian ships carrying a force of 9,000 infantry. Two weeks later he landed in front of Piombino, which was quickly besieged and then fell to the Spanish on 21 June. The same fate befell the French garrisoned town of Porto Longone. Mazarin was furious when he learned of the fall of these fortresses: his political and military actions in Italy, continuing those of his predecessor Richelieu, plus his personal pride as an Italian, were seriously damaged by the Spanish offensive. The fact that the

---

58   Israel, 'España y Europa', p.291.
59   Vincart, 'Relación de la Campaña', pp.538–539.
60   Maffi, *En Defensa del Imperio*, p.117; Pérez, 'Relación de lo Sucedido', pp.560–561; Vincart, 'Relación de la Campaña', p.541.

A cavalry clash, by print maker Theodorus van Kessel, after a design by Pieter Snayers; dated to 1656. The cavalry is without armour, except perhaps for a buff coat. While the foreground cavalryman is using his sword the man in the background is using his pistol as a club. The first infantryman defends himself with a halberd – perhaps he is a non-commissioned officer. In the background a musketeer opens fire on the horsemen, but other musketeers flee down the hill. (Rijksmuseum, Amsterdam, RP-P-OB-47.686)

Spanish Army was commanded by the competent bastard son of the Spanish King, made Mazarin's discredit even more glaring. The princes of the Italian states, faced with the news of the Spanish advance in Italy, and of the French internal conflicts and their recent defeats, were once again leaning towards Spain. Mazarin feared that the fortress of Casale, the main bastion of French power in Italy, would be the next piece to fall on the Italian chessboard. And the greatest French fear was that Savoy would make an agreement with Philip IV, because this could mean the end of a French presence in Italy, as well as making it possible for the Spanish to easily attack south-eastern France, if the Savoyards allowed the use their roads.[61]

In Catalonia, a Spanish Army from Lerida, of 6,000 men, following the course of the Ebro River, had taken Flix and besieged Tortosa. Despite the efforts of Governor General Louis de Vendôme, Duc de Mercoeur, to break the siege, the city finally surrendered on 27 November.[62]

61   Israel, 'España y Europa', p.292.
62   Israel, 'España y Europa', p.293.

In Paris, Madrid and Brussels, the exhaustion after so many years of war was palpable. During the winter of 1650–1651 rumours spread that the sovereigns had begun peace talks. This, however, was not true; Mazarin was opposed to negotiations in the existing circumstances; with France weakened and Spain seemingly regaining its power, if negotiations were to take place under these circumstances, France was in a poor negotiating position and had much to lose.[63]

As year 1651 began and the Archduke reviewed his troops, inactive since the halt to campaigning caused by the internal Dutch conflict, the Spanish infantry tercios in Flanders numbered only around 3,000 native Spaniards; even more depressing was the size of the Italian contingent at only about 700 men.

It was a very delicate situation, but France was unable to take advantage of it at the time: pressure from the nobility forced the Regent to release Condé and his friends in February 1651 and Mazarin left the Court and went into exile in the Electorate of Cologne.[64] However, his influence over the King and the Regent (Louis was still only 13) was still very strong and he advised them not to give in to any peace proposals and to reinforce the French troops in Italy, Alsace and Catalonia, especially the latter, since it remained Spain's Achilles' heel, and control of Catalonia was key to preventing Spain reinforcing other fronts. Indeed, Mazarin had revealed to his diplomats at the Münster negotiations that an occupied Catalonia could one day be exchanged for the prized Spanish Netherlands. However, the reality was quite different: by mid–1651, Philip IV controlled more than half of Catalonia, with the cities of Lleida, Tortosa, Tarragona and Vic firmly secured. France controlled only a small corridor by the sea of Cadaqués and Roses, together with the inland towns of Montblanc and Cervera and the capital of the Principality, Barcelona.[65]

Philip IV was indeed interested in achieving peace, because he felt he had a dominant position. He sent a letter to the Archduke urging him to open negotiations with France, although he insisted that the French troops should leave Catalonia – Philip IV and Mazarin agreed in their belief in the importance of Catalonia. To achieve this goal, Philip IV was prepared to offer France the counties of Roussillon and Cerdagne, Catalonian land on the other side of the Pyrenees, since it had been shown that, being on a plain, they had been definitively conquered by the French and would be again; it was thus safer to use the Pyrenees mountain range, with the stronghold fortresses of Girona and Puigcerdà as the defensive line.[66]

In Flanders, the Archduke's instructions were to take Arras. The Spanish Court had planned the campaign to capture several towns in Artois and Picardy, as a spearhead to threatening Paris; a possible minor action would be the capture of Dunkirk, to control the coastline. In Italy, the Spanish military objective was to drive the French out of the Duchy of Mantua,

63 Israel, 'España y Europa', p.294.
64 Israel, 'España y Europa', p.296; Pérez, 'Relación de lo Sucedido', p.561.
65 Israel, 'España y Europa', p.296.
66 Israel, 'España y Europa', p.297.

especially from the fortresses of Casale and Monferrato, and to detach Savoy from the French alliance. Philip IV therefore offered to return several towns and fortresses captured from the French and Savoy, the most valuable being the Savoyard frontier fortress of Vercelli, but this would only be returned to Savoy if the French had evacuated Casale.[67]

Philip IV was keen for the negotiations to bear fruit, so he appointed the efficient Conde de Fuensaldaña as diplomat plenipotentiary. The King wanted the talks to go quickly, so it would be much more practical for meetings and letters to be conducted between Paris and Brussels, rather than Paris and Madrid. Mazarin felt that the Spanish were still insufferably proud in trying to put pressure on France, even though Spain had lost numerous battles:

> The Spaniards .... behave with unparalleled insolence in the negotiation of peace, making proposals with such contempt that the last prince of Europe would be ashamed to make them.[68]

Armoured pikeman, wearing, rather unusually, long cavalry boots with spurs suggesting perhaps that Savery's 'model' was perhaps an officer – certainly spurs would be out of place for anyone serving on foot. Salomon Savery, between 1635 and 1655 (Rijksmuseum, Amsterdam)

In France, the conflict between royalty and nobility remained, but Mazarin and the other ministers, through bribery and intrigue, managed to create division and distrust among the various factions of the Fronde, especially by feeding the concern over Condé's prominence. Thus, they succeeded in getting Turenne and his elder brother, the Duc de Bouillon, to desert the Fronde for the royal side.[69] Mazarin sensed that Condé was, or would soon be, engaged in negotiations with Spain and that this was a primary reason for the 'insolence' of the Spanish authorities in Flanders.[70]

However, Mazarin's assumption that Spain was exhausted was disproved throughout 1651: in Catalonia, the Spanish took Montblanc, surrounded Barcelona and, in August 1651, began the final siege of the city by land, while a fleet of 16 warships and 23 galleys blockaded the port from the sea.

In Flanders, *Maréchal* Antoine d'Aumont de Rochebaron, Marquis de Villequier, took the strategic initiative and attacked with 30,000 men.[71] In response the Archduke and Fuensaldaña mobilised the army, while the Marqués Sfondrato, taking advantage of the attention to the two armies being elsewhere, took the opportunity to take Bourbourg and other coastal towns.[72]

The Spanish Army advanced against the French salient which threatened the Spanish Low Countries and in early September they captured Furnes, Bergues and Saint-Vinox. Mazarin believed that the next objective would be Dunkirk.[73]

67 Israel, 'España y Europa', p.299.
68 Israel, 'España y Europa', p.299.
69 Maffi, *En Defensa del Imperio*, p.220.
70 Israel, 'España y Europa', p.300.
71 Pérez, 'Relación de lo Sucedido', p.564.
72 Israel, 'España y Europa', p.301; Maffi, *En Defensa del Imperio*, p.120; Pérez, 'Relación de lo Sucedido', p.565.
73 Lonchay, *La Rivalité de la France*, p.159; Israel, 'España y Europa', p.301.

Meanwhile, Condé left Paris in September for his new post as Governor of Guiana; however, he joined the Fronde rebellion in the province and in Bordeaux, while intensifying his contacts with the Spaniards. On 6 November 1651, Condé signed an agreement with Spain by which he committed himself to provide bases and resources from the province of Gironde, and offered his collaboration by land and sea and committed himself not to negotiate with France unless he did so in the name of, or jointly with, Spain.[74] Shortly afterwards, a Spanish fleet commanded by the Baron de Batterville, sent from San Sebastian, arrived at the estuary of the Gironde and captured Talmont and the fortress of Bourg-sur-Gironde, where a garrison of Irish troops, paid by Spain and commanded by José Osorio, was installed. Condé, at the head of a small Frondist army, captured the cities of Libourne and Périgueux.[75]

Meanwhile, from Flanders the Spanish also wanted to take advantage of the momentum: Fuensaldaña assembled an army of 3,000 cavalry and 3,000 infantry to march on Paris when the Frondist nobles requested Spanish help. To distract the attention of the French defenders, the Prince de Ligne entered the Boulonnais at the head of 3,000 cavalry and 2,000 infantry.[76]

To counter Condé's change of side, Mazarin began to negotiate with Duke Charles of Lorraine, offering him the restitution of his lands in exchange for

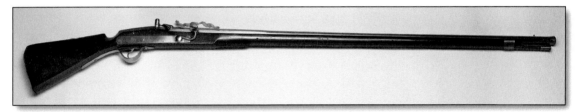

Matchlock musket. It has a round barrel, which becomes octagonal at the breech, and with a slight trumpet-shaped flare at the muzzle. Note the wooden, not steel, ramrod. The mark of the City of Utrecht is stamped on the top of the barrel and the weapon was manufactured in Utrecht, *c.* 1620–1650. Overall length is *c.* 162cm, with a calibre of 12.3mm. (Rijksmuseum. Amsterdam NG-KOG-864)

his army. Condé offered the Duke, on behalf of Spain, the handing over of the three fortresses of Stenay, Clermont and Jametz held by the Frondists in Lorraine. Mazarin urged the Court to seal an agreement with Lorraine quickly, returning the territory taken from him, except for the control of Nancy, Stenay and Marsal, which would have French garrisons to guarantee the loyalty of the fickle and ambitious Duke.[77]

The year 1652 was the year of maximum recovery of Spanish power.[78] The Fronde conflict was at its peak and the Spanish Court wished to take

---

74 Lonchay, *La Rivalité de la France*, p.159; Israel, 'España y Europa', p.302; Maffi, *En Defensa del Imperio*, p.121; Pérez, 'Relación de lo Sucedido', p.565.

75 Israel, 'España y Europa', p.302.

76 Lonchay, *La Rivalité de la France*, p.160; Maffi, *En Defensa del Imperio*, p.122; Pérez, 'Relación de lo Sucedido', p.566.

77 Israel, 'España y Europa', p.302.

78 The *Annus Mirabilis* according to Maffi, *En Defensa del Imperio*, p.126.

advantage of the French political inaction to regain the initiative in the military field and secure an advantageous position for peace negotiations that would put an end to the war. Mazarin stood in the way of peace, since, logically from the French point of view, the Cardinal was opposed to any proposal that did not recognise a French victory and their political and military supremacy. In Israel's words:

> Philip was satisfied with the victories and conquests he had achieved, but he was also determined to obtain the terms that were in keeping with his greatness and that would allow him to preserve his reputation.[79]

In January 1652 King Philip sent a message to the Archduke that he should initiate a great offensive to divert French resources to Flanders, thus enabling Spanish forces in the peninsula to conclude the siege of Barcelona without interference.[80] On 11 April the Spanish appeared in front of Gravelines: Fuensaldaña from the banks of the River Aa, followed shortly after by the Archduke from the Bourbourg area, after having captured Mardyck on 21 April. On 13 April the Spaniards annihilated a French relief column and on 17 April began the siegeworks in front of the city – it surrendered on 20 May.[81] The Spanish command now debated between besieging Dunkirk or Arras. Fuensaldaña considered that Arras should be besieged and Dunkirk blockaded by both land and sea.[82] However, from Madrid it was considered that they should enter French territory and support the Fronde, to prevent its leaders from reaching an agreement with Cardinal Mazarin – the flame of the rebellion should be kept alive in order to divide the French efforts.[83]

In Catalonia, a battlefield since 1637, most of the territory was in the hands of the Spanish Royal Army. Since 4 August 1651, Juan José of Austria had besieged Barcelona, at the head of about 2,000 cavalry and 10,000 infantry, and with a fleet of 12 galleys and several dozen smaller vessels; the defenders mustered about 6,000 men, including 3,000 French and 1,200 Swiss in the service of France. Given the political disorder inside France, Mazarin, despite his attempts to do so, was unable to effectively send reinforcements and supplies to Barcelona, or to launch a counter-offensive that could distract the Spanish troops to other fronts.[84]

In France, since January 1652 a Royalist army, made up of 6,000 German mercenaries, had begun a campaign to subdue the rebels, starting in the Loire Valley. Mazarin wanted to pacify as many provinces as possible and then move towards Paris, where the position of the Fronde was still strong, with the intention that the capital would be isolated and submit as it would then be the last of the Fronde resistance. The Royalists had defeated Condé in March in the Battle of Agen; but the Prince was confident that his troops

79   Israel, 'España y Europa', p.303.
80   Maffi, *En Defensa del Imperio*, p.122.
81   Maffi, *En Defensa del Imperio*, p.123.
82   Lonchay, *La Rivalité de la France*, p.160; Pérez, 'Relación de lo Sucedido', pp.567–569.
83   Maffi, *En Defensa del Imperio*, p.123.
84   Israel, 'España y Europa', p.303.

and his prestige could redirect the campaign towards success; that is why he advanced towards Paris; but the Duc de Lorraine also converged on the capital with his army, negotiating with Mazarin to provide his support to the Royalist side, given the deep enmity that he maintained with Condé.[85]

The Prince reached Paris, but on 2 July 1652, he suffered a massive defeat in the Parisian district of Faubourg Saint-Antoine at the hands of Turenne.[86] Condé was able to take refuge in Paris, preventing the Royalists from taking the city. When the news reached Madrid and Brussels, the Spanish Court feared that King Louis XIV had regained control, and the Archduke was therefore ordered to give priority to helping Condé rather than taking further action against the French directly.[87] Thus, the Army of Flanders, under the command of the Conde de Fuensaldaña, marched towards Paris, as Alessandro Farnese had done 60 years earlier in support of the Catholic League.[88]

The Spanish, under Fuensaldaña's command, passed through Le Câtelet and crossed the Somme to Chauny, a town which they took.[89] In response to the success of the Spanish invasion, the Duc de Lorraine changed sides and offered to collaborate with Fuensaldaña; on 20 July, the two armies joined forces, bringing their combined strength to a total of 25,000 men.[90]

In south-eastern France, a bourgeois movement known as the *Ormée* took control of Bordeaux; these merchants, shopkeepers and artisans stated their opposition to royal control, they hated Mazarin and expressed their sympathies with the Prince of Condé. In July, a Bordeaux-Frondist fleet defeated a Royalist fleet. From San Sebastian, Spain sent a fleet of 30 ships, from its Spanish, Flemish and Neapolitan squadrons. This combined anti-Royalist fleet then sailed north and attempted to capture La Rochelle, but was defeated on 9 August at the Battle of Île-de-Ré by a Royalist fleet of 26 ships and 5,300 men, commanded by the Duc de Vendôme.[91]

Undoubtedly the Spanish support was not altruistic: as in the period of the Wars of Religion and the Catholic League in the previous century, the King of Spain lent his support to the anti-royalist side as pressure to wear down the French Court. The actions of Fuensaldaña and the combined fleet were part of a strategy of weakening France in order to bring it to the negotiating table in a clearly disadvantageous position. Thus, on 21 August 1652, Philip IV sent instructions to Leopold Wilhelm to initiate diplomatic negotiations with the French for a peace.[92]

Aware that the military victories and the internal conflict had brought France to near defeat, Philip IV became very demanding in his conditions: he demanded that the French garrison of Barcelona evacuate the city immediately, in addition, he also demanded that the county of Roussillon be

85   Israel, 'España y Europa', p.304.
86   Lafuente, *Historia General*, pp.44–46.
87   Israel, 'España y Europa', p.304.
88   Pérez, 'Relación de lo Sucedido', p.569.
89   Maffi, *En Defensa del Imperio*, p.123; Pérez, 'Relación de lo Sucedido', p.569.
90   Pérez, 'Relación de lo Sucedido'; pp.570–571; Israel, 'España y Europa', p.305.
91   Israel, 'España y Europa', p.305.
92   Israel, 'España y Europa', p.306.

returned to Spanish sovereignty and, in Flanders, he demanded the return of Arras, Dunkirk and La Bassée. As the days went by, the Councillors of State expanded the list of Spanish grievances and demands adding: an end to French aid to the Portuguese rebels, restitution of the entire territory of Lorraine to Duke Charles, and that Condé and the other Frondist nobles be reinstated in all their offices and possessions. These were undoubtedly some extreme demands which some of King Philip's counsellors attempted to soften afterwards, stating that Spain would allow France to keep control of the cities of Artois and Luxembourg that had been taken by France in the 1640s (Hesdin, Thionville and Damvillers).[93]

Mazarin was not willing to give or to bend; to avoid this, he needed Barcelona to continue its resistance, and similarly he thought that France should continue to support the Portuguese war of independence. These were the two theatres of operations that contained the Spanish tide against France, while consuming the Italian human resources (Lombards, Neapolitans and Sicilians) and Spanish native troops that had traditionally flowed into Flanders and now had to be shared with the other two fronts in the Iberian Peninsula.

Mazarin knew how decisive the Spanish interior front was, and for that very reason he insisted on maintaining pressure on Catalonia; moreover, giving up Roussillon implied giving up the natural border of the Pyrenees and a territory they had already conquered, so he was not going to give in on that point; nor was he going to lose Arras, Béthune and La Bassée. And he would not give in on the rehabilitation of the rebel princes, especially Condé and Lorraine. In the words of Israel:

> Mazarin could be selfish, greedy and extremely intransigent, but he also realised, correctly, that the monarchy he served was now at a crucial juncture. In the case that the rebellion of the princes, nourished and reinforced by Spain, triumphed and succeeded in bringing the King of France to his knees, the inevitable result would be a permanent, perhaps irreversible, subordination of royal power and authority to a conjunction of internal and external forces that would relegate France to a position of structural inferiority in Europe for as long as the alliance between the princes and the Spanish Crown lasted.[94]

For Mazarin, the Fronde conflict was a return to the internal tension of the Wars of Religion of the previous century, which had removed France from the international scene for decades, to the benefit of Spain; if France gave in to the Fronde, it would return to that state. Mazarin would therefore fight at all costs to prevent this.

---

93   Israel, 'España y Europa', p.306.
94   Israel, 'España y Europa', p.307.

In Flanders, the States General had asked the Archduke to abandon the offensive actions against France, since the main objective of recovering the territory in French hands had already been achieved, and they did not want to spend more money on an action beyond their borders. Still in France was the Army of the Duc de Lorraine, whose troops sacked the province of Champagne.[95]

Nonetheless, after a few weeks, despite the reluctance of the States General of Flanders, the Archduke decided to return to campaign, since the French enemy had given ample evidence of its weakness. It was decided, therefore, to undertake the siege of Dunkirk: and the siege opened on 4 September. After repeated assaults and an intense bombardment, the garrison surrendered on 16 September; in the town the Spanish took a large amount of supplies and ammunition.[96]

In Catalonia, Mazarin ordered a relief operation for the besieged Barcelona: in mid-July a small fleet of eight ships, carrying troops and supplies, sailed from Marseilles and arrived in the waters off Barcelona on 3 August. For four days they tried to break the naval blockade by 10 galleys and several other smaller ships, but without forcing a naval battle, since the French fleet was less powerful. Unsuccessful in their attempts, on 7 August the French fleet withdrew to France. In September, the Spanish Army took the towns in the Maresme region, thus isolating Barcelona from the northern coastal lands, which cut off the land route for the supply of food and provisions which could now only arrive in small boats sailing at night in total darkness to avoid the blockade of the Spanish galleys.

Barcelona capitulated on 11 October 1652, and the next day the French troops left Barcelona. The survivors were only about 200 cavalry and 1,000 infantry, accompanied by a few Catalans, politicians who had been supportive of the French. In the following weeks, the Spanish Army advanced northwards, conquering the port of Cadaqués, besieging Roses and crossing the Pyrenees to recover territories in the counties of Roussillon and Cerdagne.[97]

The surrender of Barcelona was not the only bad news that Mazarin received. In the Italian theatre, Duca Carlo II of Mantua-Monferrato broke his alliance with France and transferred his allegiance to the Spanish. The Governor of Milan, the experienced Luis Francisco de Benavides Carrillo de Toledo, Marqués de Caracena, had promised the Duke that, if he assisted in helping the Spanish expel the French from the fortress of Casale, Spain would give him the fortress to Mantua to install a Mantuan garrison.[98]

In July 1652 the Spaniards opened the siege of Casale. After three months of intense action, in October the inhabitants of the town rose against the French and forced the garrison to retreat into the citadel, the inhabitants then opened the gates of the city so that the Spanish Army could enter. On

---

95   Israel, 'España y Europa', p.310.

96   Lonchay, *La Rivalité de la France*, p.160; Maffi, *En Defensa del Imperio*, pp.123–124; Pérez, 'Relación de lo Sucedido', p.572.

97   Israel, 'España y Europa', p.310.

98   Israel, 'España y Europa', p.309.

20 October the Spanish exploded a mine that caused a great deal of damage to the walls of the citadel and to the defenders, so that after two days the French asked to surrender. A week later, in accordance with the agreement made with the Duke of Mantua, the Spanish troops left and handed over the fortress to a Mantuan garrison, which remained for a number of years even after the end of the Franco-Spanish War in 1659.[99]

Throughout those months of 1652 the panorama had changed for France: the Spanish had triumphed in Casale, Barcelona, Gravelines and Dunkirk; and an exultant Philip IV wrote to the Archduke Leopold to entrust him with the mission of arriving at an agreed peace with France and ending the war. Additionally, the King requested the Archduke to consider and preserve the interests of the rebellious princes, especially Condé. The peace conditions offered by Spain were almost all acceptable to France: French evacuation of Catalonia, on both sides of the Pyrenees, to cut off any aid to Portugal, France would surrender Arras and most of the Artois, while Spain would hand over to France the cities of Hesdin, Thionville and Damvillers, although the French already held these. The thorniest and difficult point for Mazarin to accept would be the restitution of the independence of Lorraine and the return of the properties and rights of Condé and the other Frondist nobles, and Mazarin was unwilling to agree and to sign any peace with those conditions in the agreement.[100]

For France, if the war in Catalonia seemed already lost, the situation in Italy threatened to be even more catastrophic: especially since their Mantuan ally, who had been loyal to France for several decades, had been lost. Furthermore, the Spanish recovery in Italy seemed to be about to engulf another French ally, Savoy, so it was necessary to reinforce the French presence at the Court of Carlo Emanuele II of Savoy, a minor whose mother, Christina de Bourbon, an aunt of Louis XIV, exercised the regency despite the hostility of the King's brothers-in-law – Principe Maurizio di Savoy and his younger brother, Principe Tommaso Francesco di Saboya-Carignano, who were both supported by and supporters of Spain.[101]

Also in the month of October 1652, when Barcelona and Casale had capitulated to the Spanish armies, in France the Fronde was losing momentum at the hands of a Royalist offensive: Condé, accompanied by around 3,000 loyal men – nicknamed Condéans[102] – had to abandon Paris. They took refuge in Damvilliers,[103] but the Royalist troops continued to

---

99   Israel, 'España y Europa', p.310.
100   Israel, 'España y Europa', p.311.
101   Israel, 'España y Europa', p.312.
102   Béguin points out that Condé could only count on some of his followers, because others, despite having risen to prominence thanks to Condé's patronage during his brilliant career in the service of the French Crown, did not want to follow him into rebellion against the King. Katia Béguin, *Les Princes de Condé. Rebelles, Courtisans et Mécènes dans la France du Grand Siècle* (Seyssel: Champ Vallon, 1999), pp.23–146.
103   Pérez, 'Relación de lo Sucedido', pp.572–573.

push them towards the Spanish Netherlands:[104] then, reinforced and paid by Spain,[105] Condé took Rethel, Sainte Menehould and Bar-le-Duc.

The Archduke noted and informed Madrid that the Fronde and Condé had lost much of their support and territory in France, so they could not count on raising the people against Mazarin. At most, in the Archduke's opinion, the military experience of Condé and his troops could be used as a force to be added to the Army of Flanders, but with a limited operational capacity, due to their small numbers. In the winter of 1652–1653, Condé quartered his army in the captured strongholds and in Spanish Luxembourg.[106]

King Louis XIV, now 15 years old, had regained the centre of the country, so for 1653 Mazarin planned a campaign to reconquer the southwest and Alsace, as well as sending troops and diplomats to Italy to encourage France's Italian allies, and try to recover those who had gone over to the Spanish side.[107]

In France, Mazarin succeeded in persuading *Amiral* du Daugnon to join the royal party, by paying him a bribe of 500,000 pounds and granting him a total amnesty, the rank of *Maréchal de France* and admission into the Order of Saint Esprit. This brought Mazarin the immediate benefit of the town of Brouage and secured La Rochelle, but also offered him a victory of having restored the royal prestige, and displayed the 'magnanimity' towards those who returned to the royal obedience. It also freed more troops for the other theatres of operations: by March 1653, Royalist troops controlled almost all of southern France, only the cities of Bordeaux, Libourne, Bourg, Bergerac, Sainte Foix, Tartas and Périgueux remained in the hands of the Fronde.[108]

Faced with the Royalist advance through France, Philip IV instructed Archduke Leopold Wilhelm to resume military action from Flanders as soon as possible, with the political aim of rekindling the Frondist flame. Additionally, a plan was being prepared to bring supplies back from San Sebastian to Bordeaux, since the onset of winter had caused the fleet to withdraw to a Spanish port. Despite these plans, French Royalist troops continued to take Fronde-held positions, such as Lormont-sur-Gironde, garrisoned with 575 Irish soldiers paid for by Spain, but which surrendered to the French Royalist Army on 26 May.

---

104 Amigo highlights the fact that in French historiography, the period in which Condé was in the service of Spain is a period that it goes too far to avoid, without putting a lot of emphasis in its 'betrayal'; at the same time. Spanish historiography did not put much emphasis either on analysing the effect of a great French general being in the service of Spain. To understand the participation of Condé in the Spanish party see, Lourdes Amigo Vázquez, 'La otra imagen del héroe. El Grand Condé como aliado del rey de España (1651–1659)' in *Investigaciones Históricas, época moderna y contemporánea*, 38 (2018) and J. J. Inglish-Jones, *The Grand Condé in exiles: Power Politics in France, Spain and the Spanish Netherlands. 1652–1659*. Unpublished Doctoral thesis, University of Oxford, 1994.

105 Initially Condé was not in favour of entering the service of Spain; the Spanish politicians did not trust that plotter initially either. Experience had demonstrated to them that they could not trust the plotters who fled from Paris and arrived at Brussels with stories about plots and support for the Fronde, and of a fast victory against Louis XIV. Amigo, 'La otra imagen del héroe, p.192.

106 Galán, *La Paz de Westfalia*, p.32; Israel, 'España y Europa', p.313; Lafuente, *Historia General*, p.46.

107 Israel, 'España y Europa', p.313.

108 Israel, 'España y Europa', p.314.

The campaign of 1652 had exhausted the Army of Flanders, so it was not possible to enter into a campaign in February.[109] The theoretical strength of the Army of Flanders in March 1653, according to official figures, was 53,500 men, including both cavalry and infantry, of whom 3,545 were Spanish and 2,414 Italian.[110] The Archduke was rearming his troops and negotiating with the States General of Flanders to obtain funding for the campaign, but to no avail. On 15 June he wrote a letter to the King informing him that he could not yet open a campaign because of a lack of funds and the refusal of the States of Flanders and Brabant to give him the required funds. The two provinces were in agreement to supply money only to fund the recapture of the cities of Artois occupied by the French, but they would not provide funds for an offensive action on French soil.[111]

In addition, the Archduke also had to deal with the Prince de Condé, whose haughty character[112] frequently brought him into conflict with Spanish commanders, such as Fuensaldaña, whom Condé regarded as a subordinate. Condé knew himself to be in favour with King Philip IV and was therefore haughty and arrogant even towards the Archduke himself, who sent letters of complaint to Madrid about Condé's attitude. Condé also wrote to the King criticising the Archduke and Fuensaldaña, most especially the latter, whom he accused of hindering rather than helping him.[113] In general, Condé considered that the Spanish officers were too cautious in their preparations and actions, and moreover, Condé complained that the subsidy that King Philip IV had apportioned for him and to maintain the 3,000 soldiers in his service was being paid late.[114]

The defeat of the Fronde in 1652 allowed France to concentrate its efforts, exactly what Spain had been afraid of for many years. Mazarin ordered an offensive in Flanders, and in the middle of winter his troops recaptured Château Porcien, but could go no further.[115]

In July, the Army of Flanders re-entered France. Condé blamed the Spanish for not being prepared for the campaign until so late, and that they had chosen an inappropriate area of operations, as they had chosen to advance in the direction of Saint-Quentin, whereas Condé had suggested that it was better to march on Rethel, the objective of Turenne's campaign, which the Vicomte had taken on 8 July after a three-day siege. The Army

109 Pérez, 'Relación de lo Sucedido', p.574.
110 AGS, leg, State. 2081, 'Relación de los oficiales y soldados que ay en la infanteria y cavaleria del exercito de su Magestad en los estados de Flandes'.
111 Israel, 'España y Europa', p.316.
112 To keep Condé content, the Spanish protocol in Flanders was modified so that there was not a difference of rank between the Prince de Condé, *prince du sang*, and the General Governor of Flanders, Leopold. Amigo, 'La otra imagen del héroe, pp.191–193. As for the formal term of address, Condé was known as 'a Royal Highness', while the Archduke Leopold Wilhelm, was 'an Imperial Highness'.
113 As a matter-of-fact, the good letter-writing relationship between Philip IV and Condé, and the prestige of Condé as a general, got the King – in 1656 – to substitute Conde Fuensaldaña as Governor of the Arms of the Army of Flanders for the Marqués de Caracena, Luis Francisco de Benavides Carrillo de Toledo. Amigo, 'La otra imagen del héroe, p.196.
114 Israel, 'España y Europa', p.316.
115 Maffi, *En Defensa del Imperio*, p.126.

of Flanders, with Condé's and Lorraine's contingents, numbered 30,000, and had advanced as far as Roye and Montdidier,[116] though in Condé's opinion very slowly. Condé, according to his confidantes, claimed that the Fronde opposition to Mazarin still existed, and that it would be best to decisively advance on Paris to create a major alarm there and a sense of danger, in order to discredit Mazarin.[117]

Meanwhile, the Royalist advance continued: Bourg-sur-Gironde was invested on 4 July and surrendered two weeks later.[118] At the end of July, a royalist revolt in Bordeaux seized control of the city and opened the gates to the Royalist troops on 30 July. In August, the Prince de Conti and other Fronde leaders petitioned Mazarin for peace, and the King agreed to a pardon.

On 13 August 1653, while Turenne's army was encamped near Péronne, Condé's scouts reported their location to him and that Turenne's troops were unaware of the presence of the Spanish Army, but the bulk of the army, under

---

116 Maffi, *En Defensa del Imperio*, p.127.
117 Israel, 'España y Europa', p.316; Pérez, 'Relación de lo Sucedido', p.574.
118 Israel, 'España y Europa', p.315.

Fuensaldaña, was so late in arriving that it missed the opportunity to launch a full-scale attack. Throughout the summer the Spanish made little progress, and the capture of Rocroi on 30 September was the only tangible success – the town was garrisoned with 1,500 troops under the sole command of Condé.[119]

Given the constant disagreements between Condé and his Spanish hosts,[120] they decided to settle the disputes at a meeting. The relationship went from bad to worse and at Le Câtelet in early September, the Archduke and Condé argued more than they talked. The Archduke wrote to Philip IV about Condé's arrogant character and described how the Prince had little support in France, since the leaders and cities of the Fronde had abandoned him. The Archduke therefore requested that the King end his support for Condé or at least to reduce it, especially in the matter of subsidies. He went further and recommended that the King make peace or, on if that was not possible, substantially reinforce the army in Flanders, because the French Royalist faction was regaining the whole country and France would soon have sufficient forces to launch an offensive.[121]

King Louis XIV had indeed regained control of the whole of France by the end of the summer of 1653, but there was still widespread resentment against royal authority and especially against Cardinal Mazarin. Condé insisted to King Philip IV that the Fronde was not defeated and that France could and should still be attacked to revive the Frondist movement. Moreover, despite the French Royalist advance, Spain, and Condé, still controlled a number of important main cities – such as La Capelle, Le Câtelet, Rocroi, Stenay, Landrecies – which were not only important strongholds, but also excellent bases of operations for a direct campaign against Paris. Additionally, in Alsace, the Governor the Comte d'Harcourt was still resisting royalist attacks, to the extent that he signed an alliance with Spain and the Duc de Lorraine for them to supply him with money and troops, in return arranging the marriage of his eldest son to Lorraine's daughter and he also gave the town of Philippsburg to Lorraine.[122]

After several weeks of delay, the Spanish fleet delivered on its promise to succour Bordeaux, but it was too late. During the spring, an ambitious plan had been devised to rescue Bordeaux with a squadron and the landing of an expeditionary force, but preparations dragged on and the city surrendered to King Louis XIV. Despite this, the plan was continued with, in order to promote an uprising. To regain Bordeaux's support, Condé called for a blockade of the Gironde estuary to prevent the export of wine from the Bordeaux region and thus provoke new outbreaks of discontent with the French Crown and consequently a new rebellion.[123] The fleet, under the command of Álvaro de Bazán y Manrique de Lara, 3rd Marqués de Santa Cruz, and with Manuel Balueños as deputy commander, and composed of eight warships, eight

119 Israel, 'España y Europa', p.317; Maffi, *En Defensa del Imperio*, p.127.
120 Lafuente, *Historia General*, p.46.
121 Israel, 'España y Europa', p.317; Pérez, 'Relación de lo Sucedido', p.575.
122 Israel, 'España y Europa', p.318; Lafuente, *Historia General*, p.46.
123 Israel, 'España y Europa', p.318.

brulotes (incendiary ships) and a dozen small vessels, set sail from Cadiz and reached the mouth of the Garonne on 19 October 1653. The next day, at 3 a.m., a force landed off Mortagne-sur-Gironde to seize its fortification, while the Spanish fleet made a surprise attack on a French squadron, capturing three galleys and seven brigantines, and burning up to 30 smaller vessels. Realising that the locals would not rebel against the French King and that it would be fruitless to sail to Bordeaux, the Spaniards sacked the village of Mortagne, abandoned the area and set sail for Flanders.[124]

Meanwhile, the French launched their counter-offensive in Catalonia: an army commanded by *Maréchal* Hocquincourt, 17,000 French and exiled Catalan troops, made an invasion from Roussillon across the Pyrenees, taking Figueres and Sant Feliu de Guíxols and laying siege to Girona on 12 July. The siege lasted for 70 days until, Juan José of Austria assembled a relief force and managed to lift the siege and force the French army to retreat back to Roussillon.[125]

Throughout 1653 there had been a strategic shift against Spanish arms in Catalonia, so Philip IV ordered an assessment of which theatre of operations was the most suitable for launching an offensive against France. Once again, the idea arose of prioritising the principality of Catalonia as the main objective, but Catalonia was too devastated to maintain a field army. It was more feasible to remain on the defensive in the campaign, supporting the defence of the territory from the fortresses of Puigcerdà and Girona to stop any further French advance.[126]

Condé agreed that efforts should not be dispersed across so many fronts, and he proposed, as did the Archduke, that Flanders should be the area of the primary Spanish offensive, both as an objective in itself and to distract French resources from Catalonia or Italy. It was decided that Flanders should have the concentration of resources and the other fronts should continue with whatever resources they had. Action in France would be aimed at territorial gains and at fomenting internal dissension; overall, the aim was to get King Louis XIV to accept a 'reasonable' peace.[127]

However, the atmosphere between the generals in Flanders was not positive, quite the contrary. Condé and Fuensaldaña detested each other, and the Archduke tried to make peace, but was inclined to favour Fuensaldaña, whom he considered a faithful servant of the Crown, while he believed Condé to be too ambitious. Criticising the Archduke and Fuensaldaña, Condé warned King Philip IV that the military leadership in Flanders needed to be of the highest quality. In Israel's words, 'Condé was undoubtedly the most talented and energetic of the commanders in the Spanish Netherlands,' but Philip IV had no wish to discredit his kinsman, the Archduke, whom he confirmed as the highest authority in deciding the strategy of war in Flanders.[128]

---

124 Rodríguez, 2018, pp.879–885.
125 Israel, 'España y Europa', p.319.
126 Israel, 'España y Europa', p.319.
127 Israel, 'España y Europa', p.319.
128 Israel, 'España y Europa', p.320.

Even worse was the situation of the Duc de Lorraine, Charles IV. During the campaigns of 1653, at the height of the advance into France, he tried to negotiate on his own, both with Mazarin and with the representatives of the Fronde,[129] but entirely for his own benefit. King Philip IV, fed up with this disloyalty, ordered the Duke's arrest and, on 25 January 1654, he was arrested in Brussels and then imprisoned in the castle of Antwerp before being transferred to the prison of the Alcazar of Toledo. He subsequently remained in prison in Spain for five years, being eventually released on 15 October 1659, after the signing of the Peace of the Pyrenees.[130]

In the early months of 1654 *Maréchal* La Ferté regained control of Alsace and Count d'Harcourt submitted to royal authority in May. The next target was the Duchy of Lorraine: La Ferté's army appeared in front of the fortress of Stenay, which was occupied by Condé's supporters – the siege lasted until 6 August, when the fortress surrendered to the French.[131] Condé, however, wished to save the city, but both the Archduke and Fuensaldaña were unwilling to risk the army to save Stenay. At Condé's insistence, the Archduke decided to attack France at Artois, with the city of Arras as his objective, even though the city had a garrison of 5,000 men.[132]

French spies reported that the Spanish Army, 22,000 men strong – 10,000 cavalry and 12,000 infantry[133] – had no intention of coming to Lorraine's aid, so Turenne was asked to reinforce Arras. The Spanish Army opened the siege of Arras on 2 July, which continued throughout August, until on 25 August Turenne launched a furious assault that allowed him to break the Spanish lines, forcing a hasty retreat of the entire Spanish Army. The retreat would have turned into a major disaster had it not been for the courageous action of Condé,[134] who managed to save much of the army. Turenne, however, captured over 3,000 men, 900 horses and 60 plus guns of all types, as well as large quantities of supplies. The Archduke was forced to retreat with a few hundred men to Douai, while Condé – with most of the Spanish cavalry and infantry and cavalry – retreated to Cambrai, and Fuensaldaña went with his escort to Valenciennes. As a result of this defeat, Turenne also took Le Quesnoy from the Spanish.[135]

That defeat had been the first since Lens in 1648 and damaged the morale of the Army of Flanders, which had maintained the strategic initiative which had allowed it to invade France on several occasions, despite a lack of resources.[136] This victory damaged Condé's prestige in France, but it won him

129 Lafuente, *Historia General*, p.46.
130 Israel, 'España y Europa', p.326.
131 Maffi, *En Defensa del Imperio*, p.129.
132 Maffi, *En Defensa del Imperio*, p.129.
133 Lafuente, *Historia General*, p.51.
134 Amigo notes that Condé's personal attendance was highly sought after at the Madrid Court and that, since then, the esteem for Condé had greatly increased. Amigo, 'La otra imagen', p.194.
135 Lafuente, *Historia General*, p.51.
136 Lonchay, *La Rivalité de la France*, p.167; Maffi, *En Defensa del Imperio*, p.130.

A cavalry battle, published by Lucas Vorsterman after a design by Jacques Courtois Le Bourguignon. The engraving was made in Antwerp, c. 1651/1652. The cavalry is fighting with pistol and sword. Some wear helmets, but most wear a wide hat, often decorated with a feather, most wear a buff coat and *may* also have back and breast. (Rijksmuseum. RP-P-OB-61.730)

a great deal of recognition in Flanders and Madrid, since it was thanks to him that the army had been saved.[137]

Archduke Leopold Wilhelm was exhausted but also disgusted with Condé and the infighting among the generals of the Army of Flanders, so he requested King Philip to allow him to step down as Governor General.[138]

Curiously, Condé's brother, the Prince de Conti, was gaining ascendancy at the French Court: after reconciling with the King and Mazarin, he had been appointed viceroy of Catalonia in May 1654. In July he launched a campaign from Perpignan to recover all the Spanish territories on that side of the Pyrenees; and in September he invaded Cerdagne and laid siege to Puigcerdà, which was defended by 1,000 Italian, German and Catalan soldiers; the town surrendered on 21 September. In the following weeks, the French and their Catalan allies reconquered the rest of Cerdagne.[139]

---

137 Amigo, 'La otra imagen del héroe, p.192, p.210, Israel, 'España y Europa', p.321; Lonchay, *La Rivalité de la France*, p.167; Inglis-Jones, 1994, pp.75–116.

138 Lafuente, *Historia General*, p 51.

139 Israel, 'España y Europa', p 322.

Mazarin also tried to undermine Spanish power in Italy. A powerful French fleet sailed from Toulon in early November and on 14 November seized the port of Castellammare in the Gulf of Naples: their intention was to encourage a new anti-Spanish uprising, like that of 1647–1648. They received little local support, however, and were defeated by the Spanish troops stationed in Naples.[140]

On the international stage, England defeated The United Provinces in 1654 (The First Anglo-Dutch War). Both France and Spain[141] had negotiated with England to bring it over to their side; the Madrid Court tempted England with a cash subsidy but refused to make trade concessions; the negotiations failed. In return for English aid, the French agreed to withdraw support for the exiled Charles II of England, who, with his supporters then joined the Army of Flanders. France also agreed to give economic and territorial compensation to the English. Cromwell preferred to ally with Catholic France to jointly defeat Catholic Spain,[142] which at the time did not have a fleet strong enough to keep maritime communications with America and Flanders open and secure.[143]

During the winter of 1654/1655, Mazarin sounded out the Spanish authorities for peace talks; and on this occasion, his demands seemed reasonable to the Spanish Crown: France would return to Spain the towns of Béthune, La Bassée, Le Quesnoy, Thionville and Damvillers, in exchange for the Spanish surrendering La Capelle, Le Câtelet, Rocroi, Arras, Hesdin and Bapaume. Additionally, France would evacuate Catalonia and give no further aid to the Catalan and Portuguese rebels, in exchange for retaining possession of the county of Roussillon. However, with regard to the new Duc Nicolas-François de Lorraine and the Prince de Condé, Mazarin was not so generous: the Duke was offered only financial compensation, but no guarantee of restitution of his duchy or his sovereignty; and Condé was offered only vague promises of satisfaction. Mazarin had calculated that both princes would reject this peace offer. Archduke Leopold Wilhelm tried to convince King Philip IV of the necessity of concluding peace, despite the compromise with Condé and Lorraine, that reasons of state took precedence and that it was necessary to preserve the Spanish Netherlands, since these provinces were too exhausted to continue the war. However, neither the King nor his *valido*, Luis de Haro,[144] nor some of his chief advisers, agreed, because

---

140 Israel, 'España y Europa', p 322.

141 See Porfirio Sanz Camañes, 'Conveniencia política y pragmatismo religioso en las relaciones entre Felipe IV y Cromwell' in *Tiempo de cambios: guerra, diplomacia y política internacional de la Monarquía Hispánica (1648–1700)*, (Madrid: Actas, 2012), pp.311–340.

142 Lafuente comments on two incidents that provoked Cromwell's enmity: the assassination in Madrid of his ambassador by Royalist supporters and the quarrel in London between the French and Spanish embassies over who had precedence within the diplomatic corps accredited to England. Lafuente, *Historia General*, pp.53–54.

143 Galán, *La Paz de Westfalia*, p 33; Lonchay, *La Rivalité de la France*, p.170.

144 About this politician and diplomat, see R. Valladares (ed.), *El Mundo de un Valido. Don Luis de Haro y su Entorno, 1643–1661* (Madrid, Marcial Pons, 2016) and A. Malcolm, *Royal Favouritism and the Governing Elite of the Spanish Monarchy 1640–1665* (Oxford: OUP, 2017).

of the loss of international reputation that abandoning their 'allies' would entail.[145] So, the war went on.[146]

Spain, fighting on so many fronts, was becoming increasingly exhausted. Genoa, the former political and financial ally, was increasingly at odds with Spain. And without loans, the King of Spain could not pay his soldiers, recruit new troops nor compensate his allies.[147]

In the spring, Condé's brother, Prince de Conti, attacked Catalonia again and expanded French rule, securing Roses and taking Cadaqués on 27 May 1655. A few weeks later, in Flanders, a French army under Turenne and La Ferté laid siege to Landrecies. And in Italy, a Franco-Savoyard army entered Lombardy and laid siege to Pavia. This was all part of a great all-out French offensive on all fronts, but the highly competent Marqués de Caracena, Governor and Captain General of the Milanese territory, led an army out of Milan and defeated the French, liberating Pavia.[148]

Spain was approaching collapse; the Court secretly sent Pedro de Vaus to meet Mazarin at Soissons on 3 July 1655. The Cardinal was explicit: Condé was the problem, otherwise the claims of both sides at the recent peace talks were reasonable for both countries. Mazarin said he did not understand Philip IV's insistence on maintaining his support for Condé and for Lorraine, and gave as an example that Louis XIV was prepared to withdraw support from the pretender to the throne of Portugal, the Duque de Braganza, who had been proclaimed King João IV, if Philip IV would do the same for Mazarin's antagonists. The Cardinal insisted that Condé was more of a hindrance to Spain, since his army was paid for by Spain and had become mercenaries without ideals.

Mazarin outlined the advantages of peace and described the threats to Spain: the French recovery in Catalonia, the advance in Flanders and the growing threat from the English.[149] As for the latter, Cromwell had planned to attack Spanish possessions in the Americas, putting his 'Western Design' into practice. In December 1654, a powerful fleet under Admiral William Penn and Commander Robert Venables, consisting of 17 warships and 20 transports, carrying 325 guns, 1,145 sailors and 1,830 soldiers, sailed for the Caribbean with the aim of capturing the island of Hispaniola, but the attack in April 1655 failed. The English fleet then proceeded to Jamaica on 21 May and succeeded in taking it.[150]

For the campaign of 1655, the Archduke lamented that he had no money to maintain his troops and to buy supplies. In March he still did not have the supplies for his army, and so he wrote to Madrid asking for permission

---

145 About whether the privileges of Condé were really an impediment or an excuse to continue the war, see Amigo, 'La otra imagen del héroe, pp.197–199.
146 Israel, 'España y Europa', p.322.
147 Israel, 'España y Europa', p.324.
148 Israel, 'España y Europa', p.324.
149 Galán, *La Paz de Westfalia*, p.33; Israel, 'España y Europa', p.325.
150 C. Black, *The Story of Jamaica from Prehistory to the Present* (London: Collins, 1965), pp.46–50; Lonchay, *La Rivalité de la France*, p.171; Valladares, 1998, pp.142–144. For a more exhaustive information of the campaign: Gardina, Carla: *The English Conquest of Jamaica*, The Belknap Press, Harvard, 2017.

to request a local truce in Flanders, a proposal rejected by the *valido* Luis de Haro, who insisted on keeping the Flanders theatre of operations active.[151]

Reluctantly, in early June the Archduke concentrated his forces, around 20,000 strong, at Tournai, but remained there without advancing, because of the lack of resources. In May, Condé and his troops attempted to seize Le Quesnoy, but Turenne prevented them and seized Le Câtelet.[152]

Instead, Turenne launched his offensive: the Viscount army of 16,000 men and La Ferté's army of 10,000 men converged on Landrecies, and they opened the siege on 18 June. The Archduke did not have the resources to support the town, nor did he want to risk the army in a pitched battle, so he sent cavalry detachments to plunder French towns and harass the supply convoys for the besiegers. Landrecies, defended by a garrison of 2,000, surrendered on 14 July. This surprised the Archduke and his generals, who were confident that the strong garrison would hold out longer. Turenne then laid siege to La Capelle, which was defended by Condé's troops. The Archduke moved the army to avoid a second defeat and the French withdrew.[153]

Even with the bad news from Flanders, Philip IV and his ministers were convinced that Mazarin was insincere, and that there was no reason for a peace that was safe and dignified. The King wrote to the Archduke informing him that he intended to negotiate with France, and that he would defend Condé's interests, provided they were not excessive; he also stated that he disliked the Duc de Lorraine more, since it was known that he, like his brother Charles, had repeatedly negotiated with Mazarin, and his loyalty was questionable, fearing that he would abandon the alliance with Spain if the Cardinal offered him some crumbs.

Philip IV, despite keeping Duc Charles in prison, was interested in safeguarding the integrity of the Duchy of Lorraine, as a buffer state between France and The Empire, and as a base of operations from which to threaten French power. Mazarin's aim was quite the opposite, to secure the Duchy under French power, and thus he insisted that the Duchy was a possession of France and that the brothers Charles and Nicolas-François of Lorraine, in going to war against the Kings of France, had acted not as a sovereign state but as rebels.[154]

Philip IV was suspicious of Mazarin's proposals regarding Catalonia, since he did not promise to withdraw from Catalonia given that French troops had occupied Roses and Cadaqués. In Flanders, Mazarin did not offer to return the captured towns of Artois. Philip IV, in a letter to the Archduke, explained that he was confident that God and Fortune could turn the tide of war around again; just a year earlier it seemed that France was on its knees.

According to Philip IV, both Spain and Flanders were exhausted, humanly and economically, but so also was France: its subjects were tired of the enormous fiscal pressure, and all this meant that there were more and more people becoming discontent and becoming supporters of the Fronde. Philip

---

151 Maffi, *En Defensa del Imperio*, pp.133–134.
152 Lafuente, *Historia General*, p.51.
153 Lafuente, *Historia General*, p.51; Maffi, *En Defensa del Imperio*, p.134.
154 Israel, 'España y Europa', p.326.

IV therefore encouraged the Archduke to be optimistic about the future. But the Archduke was in Flanders, on the front line, and he knew the limitations faced in the war: there were few Spaniards and Italians among the troops and the defences were not adequate to withstand prolonged sieges. He had to break up his army to prevent any surprise attacks such as that of Landrecies, sending troops to Charlemont, Namur, et cetera.[155]

Turenne captured Condé on 17 August, and Saint-Ghislain on 25 August. The French Army continued its advance, threatening to take L'Escluse, Valenciennes, Cambrai and Tournai. The deep advance left the French lines of communication very exposed and the Spanish cavalry attacked the supply convoys; eventually Turenne, leaving strong garrisons in the captured towns, withdrew to France in October 1655.[156]

That summer, the French continued to campaign in Catalonia, trying to extend their zone of dominance to the south and along the coast to guarantee supplies, in pursuance of which they laid siege to Palamós. However, in September the Spanish managed to bring a fleet close in to the seaside town, forcing the French to lift the siege.[157]

Philip IV was counting on the loyalty of Condé to continue to resist the onslaught of Louis XIV's armies. It remained, however, to secure the loyalty of the two Lorraine brothers: one was a prisoner in Toledo, while the serving was in Flanders. The King of Spain negotiated with them for the Lorrainer Army to be integrated into the Army of Flanders, form part of the same command, and to be under the same discipline and pay structure as the King's troops. Additionally, the Duke would undertake not to sign a separate peace with France and in return, once the Lorrainer regiments were incorporated into his Army, Philip IV would compensate the Duke with land and money and grant Charles his freedom.[158]

However, the Duke refused to accede to these demands and Philip kept him imprisoned. The Duke was so offended by the captivity and by Philip IV's mistrust, and in turn the latter was convinced that the Duke would go over to the French as soon as he had the opportunity, that Philip IV decided not to release him. In Flanders, Duc Nicolas-François went over to the French with most of his army in November 1655, and the following year, the Lorrainers fought against their former Spanish allies.[159]

In early 1656 a new Governor General arrived in Flanders: King Philip IV had appointed his illegitimate son Juan José of Austria, with the mission of turning the tide of war. As with Philip II and his bastard brother Juan de Austria, the illegitimate son of Charles V and Barbara Blomberg,[160] the relationship between Philip IV and Juan José was peculiar: it was a love-hate relationship. Both loved each other, but there was also jealousy and fear between them: Juan José had the military skills that his crowned father lacked

155 Maffi, *En Defensa del Imperio*, p.135.
156 Israel, 'España y Europa', p.327; Maffi, *En Defensa del Imperio*, p.135.
157 Israel, 'España y Europa', p.327.
158 Israel, 'España y Europa', p.328.
159 Israel, 'España y Europa', p.329.
160 Lafuente, *Historia General*, p.51.

and he had served his father well in Catalonia and Italy. However, King Philip could not consider Juan José as his heir because he was illegitimate, and thus always sought a legitimate male heir, the son of the King and a European princess. On 15 April 1656, Juan José wrote to the King of the dire military and economic situation in Flanders, and asked his father to sign a peace with France to preserve the dominions he still possessed.[161]

In early summer, the French army of 8,000 cavalry and 17,000 infantry under Turenne attacked again, pushing beyond Douai and Cambrai, and on 15 June 1656 laid siege to Valenciennes, which was bombarded by artillery for a month. However, on the night of 15 July, the Army of Flanders, 8,000 cavalry and 12,000 infantry under Juan José and the Prince de Condé, appeared behind the French lines. The French Prince's relationship with his Spanish counterpart was much more cordial than that with Archduke Leopold Wilhelm. The Spaniard broke through the French defensive line, causing Turenne's army to panic: it was a repeat, in reverse, of the Battle of Arras two years earlier. The Spanish inflicted on the French around 4,000 dead and wounded, and took perhaps as many as 4,000 prisoners, including *Maréchal* La Ferté, as well as a large quantity of materiel and supplies, including the siege train of 50 guns, all at a cost of only 500 Spanish casualties, dead and wounded. This Spanish victory, largely due to Condé's military genius, restored Spain's prestige in Europe at a time when France's rise was thought to be unstoppable. Turenne received orders from Mazarin to halt the Spanish advance, but was unable to prevent the Spanish from capturing the town of Condé on 20 July. The victories were widely celebrated in the Spanish Netherlands and in Madrid.[162]

The Army of Flanders entered Picardy, razing more than 300 villages and forcing Turenne's army to take cover in Saint-Quentin; the Spanish plundered French territory until September, when they returned to Flanders.[163]

It was then that peace negotiations resumed in earnest: France reiterated its willingness to withdraw from all of Catalonia and to return Cerdagne, but would retain Roussillon; they would also withdraw support for the Portuguese rebels; in exchange, the Spanish would accept the ceding of Alsace to France. The problem now lay in Flanders: the French had managed to retain much of the previous year's conquests, and were unwilling to give that up. After much negotiation and tension, Philip IV agreed to cede the province of Artois and to return the fortified towns of Rocroi, La Capelle and Le Câtelet. In return, France would return the towns of Thionville and Damvillers in Luxembourg, Béthune, Le Quesnoy and La Bassée in Flanders. Additionally, France would withdraw from Charolais and those parts of Spanish Burgundy which they held. In Lorraine, France agreed to the return of the dukes, who would enjoy full sovereignty, but in return had to cede to the French the Duchy of Bar, guarantee them a corridor to connect with French Alsace and, in addition –

---

161 Galán, *La Paz de Westfalia*, p.33; Israel, 'España y Europa', p.329; Maffi, *En Defensa del Imperio*, p.137.
162 Amigo, 'La otra imagen', pp.188–189; Galán, *La Paz de Westfalia*, p.33; Israel, 'España y Europa', p.330; Lafuente, *Historia General*, p.52; Maffi, *En Defensa del Imperio*, p.138.
163 Maffi, *En Defensa del Imperio*, p.139.

this being a very thorny issue – the important city of Nancy was to demolish its walls. In Italy, Spain would return Vercelli to Savoy. However, a major stumbling block was deciding who would get the strategic stronghold of Casale, wanted by all the contenders on the Italian chessboard. It was finally agreed that Casale should be demilitarised and its walls demolished, but there no agreement was reached was on the delineation of the zones of influence in Mantua and Modena.[164]

These proposals were initially accepted by Spain, which agreed to recognise French control over Artois and Alsace, and which would return the towns of Rocroi and Le Câtelet to France.

Condé had regained his position at the Court in Brussels since the arrival of Juan José of Austria, and also his position in relation to the Court in Madrid. Mazarin was informed of this situation and of Condé's power and ascendancy in Spain's military decision-making, to such an extent that the Cardinal was convinced that Condé, with these successes, was aiming for the creation of a plan aimed at a general discontent against Mazarin that would help to revive the Fronde.[165]

Condé knew from his spies that Mazarin sought to make Philip IV discontent with Condé, and he also knew that the Cardinal sought to foster the idea that Condé's personal interests were to blame for the lack of progress in the negotiations. The Prince was not mistaken, since when the Spanish negotiators raised the subject of Condé's claims, Mazarin rejected them out of hand, claiming that they would deal with them only after other agreements had been reached. As the negotiations progressed and the Condé question began to be discussed, Mazarin undertook only to restore Condé's property that had been seized, but not to restore him to his offices and to his influence at Court.

Philip IV rejected these overtures about Condé; he did so not only to keep his promise to the prince and for international prestige, but also because he feared that, if Condé returned to the French Court, he would lose all influence with the prince. However, he also feared that all the knowledge Condé had acquired about the weaknesses in Flanders would be turned against Spain. Mazarin made an offer of a marriage alliance between the two kingdoms to seal a definitive peace: King Louis XIV wished to marry the Infanta Maria Teresa, daughter of the King of Spain and at the time heir to her father, since the death of her brothers. This could mean that the two kingdoms would be united in a single Crown, under the sceptre of Louis XIV, and King Philip IV thus refused.[166] Mazarin was able to manage the negotiations so that internationally the failure was blamed on Spain and Condé, although everything had been orchestrated by the Cardinal to bring the negotiations to an inconclusive end.[167]

Spain regained the initiative in the campaign of 1657, following the French defeat of the previous year. The Spanish Army opened the siege of

164 Galán, *La Paz de Westfalia*, p.33; Israel, 'España y Europa', p.332.
165 Israel, 'España y Europa', p.334.
166 Israel, 'España y Europa', p.334.
167 Israel, 'España y Europa', p.333.

Saint-Ghislain on 15 March, and on 23 March the city surrendered.[168] On 23 March, France and England signed a new alliance, agreeing to take the coastal cities of Flanders (Gravelines, Mardyck and Dunkirk), with a force of 26,000 men – 20,000 French and 6,000 English – supported by an English fleet; England would retain the cities of Dunkirk and Mardyck.[169] When Philip IV learned of the treaty, he ordered the confiscation of all English ships and goods in Spain, and forbade all trade with England, as he had done with France, with Portugal, and with all enemy powers.[170]

To put pressure on Flanders' resources with a broad front, the French decided to attack through Luxembourg and Flanders. La Ferté moved at the head of 20,000 men against the fortress of Montmédy, defended by Jean d'Allamont de Malandry in command of a garrison of around 600 men. The fortress held out for over 6 weeks and after Allamont was killed and the garrison realised that no relief would be forthcoming, the citadel finally surrendered on 6 August.[171]

In Flanders, Turenne, with 24,000 men, opened the siege of Cambrai on 29 May,[172] but on the 31st Condé arrived at the head of a detachment of 4,000 cavalry and managed to enter the city. Condé's force was the vanguard of the Spanish Army, and thus Turenne decided to lift the siege.[173] It seemed that the Army of Flanders had been reborn and could march on Paris at will, but then a reinforcement arrived – 6,000 men of the English Army.[174]

Over the next few weeks, the two sides troops barely moved. Cromwell pressed Mazarin to honour the agreements of March 1657 and Turenne besieged Saint-Venant on 16 August; it surrendered on 27 August.[175] From there the Anglo-French forces opened the siege of Mardyck, defended by Juan de la Torre, on 29 September. Mardyck surrendered on 3 October. Turenne explored the possibilities of besieging Gravelines or Dunkirk, but the area around the former had been flooded and it was impossible to approach, while the latter had been reinforced, so further attacks on the area were abandoned.[176]

English naval cooperation was also successful: in September the ships under the English Admiral Robert Blake captured part of the fleet of the 'Treasure of the Indies', with the result that Madrid had no money to send to Flanders and its other territories. Juan José of Austria, faced with the urgency of having to have an army to be able to confront the Anglo-French forces, but with no money to recruit troops, asked for battalions to be sent from the Iberian Peninsula in Dutch ships – The United Provinces were officially

168 Israel, 'España y Europa', p.334; Maffi, *En Defensa del Imperio*, p.143.
169 Lafuente, *Historia General*, p.54; Lonchay, *La Rivalité de la France*, p.171.
170 Lafuente, *Historia General*, p.54.
171 Louis XIV entered into the citadel and paid tribute to Allamont's bravery (Lonchay, *La Rivalité de la France*, p.171).
172 Maffi, *En Defensa del Imperio*, p.143.
173 Lafuente, *Historia General*, p.52; Lonchay, *La Rivalité de la France*, p.171; Maffi, *En Defensa del Imperio*, p .143
174 Lafuente, *Historia General*, p.55.
175 Lafuente, *Historia General*, p.55; Maffi, *En Defensa del Imperio*, p.144.
176 Lonchay, *La Rivalité de la France*, p.172; Maffi, *En Defensa del Imperio*, p.145.

Aerial view of Gravelines today. The Gravelines fortress was improved throughout the sixteenth and seventeenth centuries; for decades before Vauban made the *Trace Italienne* 'famous' Spanish, Italian, Walloon and Dutch military engineers built imposing bastioned fortifications. In this aerial view the so-called star shaped system of defences, with successive bastions and redoubts, can easily be seen – here also taking advantage of the course of the river. (Google maps)

neutral, but with a grudge against the French and English – but the Council of State could not send troops without losing protection for Catalonia or other peninsular territories,[177] thus it preferred to send bills of exchange so that troops could be recruited in Flanders and Germany.

There were difficulties in collecting the bills given the Crown's difficult financial situation – lenders were no longer willing to lend money, as they thought they would not be repaid, and they would only lend small amounts while demanding very high interest. Thus the bills of exchange raised hardly any funds, and as a result Juan José was forced to raise taxes, which led to disturbances in Flanders and complaints from the Franche-Comté authorities, who had always enjoyed important privileges over taxation.[178]

To try to create a distraction and divert English attention and thus aid, Madrid considered funding a Stuart expedition to Scotland in order to reduce the pressure on Flanders. However, Governor Juan José refused to cooperate with the idea, demanding that all of the, albeit meagre, resources be directed to Flanders, with the intention of recapturing Mardyck and of protecting Dunkirk. The plan to invade Scotland was scrapped, but Flanders did not receive the money and resources it needed to defend itself either.[179]

The Spanish Court also tried to break the Anglo-French alliance, offering Cromwell the town of Calais, but the Lord Protector remained faithful to his commitment to Mazarin and on 28 March 1658 the two powers even renewed their alliance.[180]

Despite the lack of resources, Juan José of Austria launched a small offensive, which enabled him to capture Hesdin, thanks to the French

177 Galán, *La Paz de Westfalia*, p.33.
178 Galán, *La Paz de Westfalia*, p.33.
179 Galán, *La Paz de Westfalia*, p.32.
180 Lonchay, *La Rivalité de la France*, p.172.

governor switching to the Spanish side, and then defeat the relief columns under *Maréchal* Hocquincourt at Hesdin in April, and *Maréchal* d'Aumont at Ostend in May.[181]

The alliance between France and England led, in 1658, to a joint offensive against the Spanish Netherlands. The Anglo-French troops advanced rapidly towards Dunkirk on 25 May.[182] The town was defended by 800 cavalry and 2,200 infantry under the command of the Marqués de Lede. On 13 June, the Army of Flanders, commanded by Juan José of Austria and the Prince de Condé, advanced to relieve the town in a forced march that left the troops exhausted and without their artillery and baggage train, which were left far behind.

On 14 June 1658, the two armies met at the Battle of the Dunes of Leffrinckoucke:[183] Turenne commanded an army of 9,000 cavalry and 6,000 infantry. Juan José had 6,000 cavalry and 8,000 infantry, divided into two groups: the right wing, the Spanish troops, and the left wing, commanded by Condé, with Swiss, Irish and English troops loyal to King Charles II, led by his brother, the Duke of York, the future James II of England. Condé's flank held out, but the Spanish flank was defeated. On the field, the courage and professionalism of the English contingent from the erstwhile New Model Army stood out.

The Spanish Army left 1,000 dead, 3,000 wounded on the field and also lost some 4,000 prisoners. The Anglo-French suffered less than 1,000 casualties in all.[184] The defeat meant that the city of Dunkirk fell on 24 June, and by virtue of the Anglo-French agreement, it was passed into British hands; the French advanced along the coast and took Gravelines, Furnes, Diksmuide and Ypres.[185] The defeat on the battlefield also broke the defensive system of Flanders that had resisted for so many years.

The Allies continued to advance eastwards, as the defeat of the Army of Flanders at the Dunes had been so resounding: some Spanish historians believe that it was the Battle of the Dunes, not the Battle of Rocroi, that marked the end of the supremacy of the Spanish tercios. By the autumn of 1658 barely a third of the Flemish territory remained in Spanish hands. Only English disinterest in continuing the campaign in a territory alien to their geopolitical objectives and the military and economic exhaustion of France saved Spain from total defeat in Flanders.[186]

Juan José of Austria wrote to Philip IV about the delicate situation in Flanders, as the French army was now free to occupy the whole territory.[187] Philip IV requested a truce, which Mazarin refused, believing that success

---

181 Maffi, *En Defensa del Imperio*, p.148.

182 Lonchay, *La Rivalité de la France*, p.173; Maffi, *En Defensa del Imperio*, p.149.

183 Galán, *La Paz de Westfalia*, p.34; Lafuente, *Historia General*, p.55; Lonchay, *La Rivalité de la France*, pp.173–175. For a more in-depth knowledge of this battle: Inglish-Jones, 1994, pp.249–277.

184 Michael Clodfelter, *Warfare and Armed Conflicts: A Statistical Encyclopedia of Casualty and Other Figures, 1492–2015* (Jefferson: McFarland, 2017).

185 Galán, *La Paz de Westfalia*, p.34; Lonchay, *La Rivalité de la France*, pp.173–175; Maffi, *En Defensa del Imperio*, pp.149–150.

186 Galán, *La Paz de Westfalia*, p.34.

187 Maffi, *En Defensa del Imperio*, p.150.

was within his grasp. But on 15 August, Spain won an important victory at Camprodon in Catalonia; the death of Cromwell in September caused instability in England and a retreat of the French Army; and in Northern Italy peace came when the French allies, Savoy and Modena, agreed to a truce with the Spanish Viceroy, Marqués de Caracena.[188]

The political-military scenario had changed for France, and it was no longer so favourable, but Spain had been dealt a severe blow and was clearly weak: the Portuguese had just launched a powerful offensive and the war on so many fronts seemed impossible to sustain, for the lack of both troops and money.

Both France and Spain now wished to end hostilities and reach a peace that would put an end to almost a decade and a half of constant warfare. Philip IV now had a male heir, Prince Philip Prospero born in 1657, and a second son, the Infant Ferdinand Thomas born in 1658 (sadly the two princes died in 1661 and 1659 respectively) and thus the fear that his daughter Maria Teresa would be the heir and transmit the Crown of Spain to Louis XIV or his heirs disappeared. In fact, the Infanta was betrothed to Archduke Leopold, son of Emperor Ferdinand III, but it was finally agreed that she would marry Louis XIV to seal the peace. Leopold, in order to maintain the alliance with his Spanish cousins, in 1666 married another of Philip IV's daughters, Margarita Teresa of Austria.[189]

Philip IV had a third son, Prince Carlos, who was born in 1661. Philip was the maternal uncle of his wife, Princess Mariana of Austria (Habsburg) and at the time, both Philip and Marian were descendants of a continual intermarriage between the Spanish and the Austrian lines of the Habsburg family. No doubt this affected Prince Carlos, probably as well as his other brothers and sisters, and Prince Carlos always had health problems. It has been suggested that the child suffered from Klinefelter's syndrome, and by others that he had Fragile X syndrome.[190] Whatever the case, his life was hard, surrounded by doctors, and his death on 1 November 1700 provoked a dynastic crisis and caused the outbreak of the War of the Spanish Succession (1701–1715).[191]

---

188 Galán, *La Paz de Westfalia*, p.34.
189 Galán, *La Paz de Westfalia*, p.34.
190 When the Prince became King, he was known as *El Hechizado* (The Bewitched), because of his constant ill health and the numerous medical and healing procedures that were performed on him. G. Álvarez, F. C. Ceballos, C. Quintero, 'El 'hechizo' genético de Carlos II', in *Investigación y Ciencia* (403), pp.10–11; E. Navalón Ramón, Ferrando Lucas, MT.: 'La enfermedad de Carlos II', in *Revista Valenciana de Medicina de Familia (RVMF)*, Nº 22, 10(2), 2006, pp.16–19.
191 1701–1714 in Great Britain.

8

The Peace

In November 1657 King Philip IV had sent the Spanish diplomat Antonio Pimentel to initiate secret peace talks with Mazarin.[1] While the war still seemed likely to be resolved in Spain's favour; between January and May 1658 the two politicians were negotiating the main points of a future peace agreement. Peace negotiations between the two crowns were officially opened on the Isla de los Faisanes in July 1659, between Luis de Haro, Philip IV's favourite (*valido*), and Cardinal Mazarin.[2]

Spain, in its conflict with France, had managed to invade French territory during the command of *Cardinal-Infante* Ferdinand of Austria, Governor of Flanders from 1634–1641. In later periods, such as Melo's campaign that culminated at Rocroi on 19 May 1643 or Archduke Leopold's campaigns of 1648–1654, Spain now found that it had lost control of important places in the west and south of Flanders and Luxembourg: Gravelines, Mardyck, Dunkirk, Courtrai, Bergues, Saint Winoc, Furnes, almost all of Artois, Arras, Hesdin, Lens, Béthune, La Bassée, Thionville and Damvillers.[3]

The Treaty of the Pyrenees, signed on 7 November 1659 between the two great Catholic monarchies, put an end to the armed confrontation between France and Spain. The 124 article treaty established very advantageous peace terms for France. On its northern border, France received the county of Artois except for Aire-sur-la-Lys, Arques, Clairmarais and Saint-Omer, as well as a number of strongholds in Flanders, Hainaut and Luxembourg: Avesnes-sur-Helpe, Bourbourg, Carignan, Chauvency-le-Château, Damvillers, Gravelines, Landrecies, Le Quesnoy, Marville, Metz, Montmédy, Philippeville, Saint-Venant, Thionville, Toul and Verdun. The French returned Charolais – in Franche-Comté – and its Italian conquests of Cassano d'Adda, Mortara, Valenza and Vigevano to Spain. Spain returned Vercelli to Savoy. France returned the Duchy of Lorraine to its sovereign Charles IV, but kept the towns of Stenay and Clermont-en-Argonne. Later, by the Treaty of Vincennes in 1661, Charles was given back the Duché de Bar,

---

1   For a summary of the several negotiating rounds between the two powers from the Peace of Westphalia 1648 see, Israel, 'España y Europa', pp.273–281.

2   Galán, *La Paz de Westfalia*, p.34.

3   Israel, 'España y Europa', p.280; Lonchay, *La Rivalité de la France*, pp.175–179.

except for the towns of Héming, Réding, Sarrebourg and Sierck-les-Bains, which remained in French hands.[4]

On the French southern border, the French withdrew from their conquests in Cadaqués, Castelló d'Empúries, Puigcerdà and Roses. Spain had to cede the counties of Roussillon, Conflent, Vallespir and part of the Cerdagne region, all of which were located north of the Pyrenees and which French troops had occupied in support of the Catalan rebels. The border with Spain was henceforth set along the Pyrenees, except for the Aran Valley, which faced north of the Pyrenees.[5] The Treaty established that 33 villages in the County of Cerdagne would be ceded to France: these would be defined in 1660 at the Ceret Conference and in the definitive Treaty of Llívia, which definitively delimited the new border between the territories of the two crowns and where Philip IV's negotiators managed to retain Llívia on the grounds that it was a town and not a village, due to it being granted the status and title of 'town' by The Emperor Charles V in 1528.[6]

The Treaty also provided for the marriage between Louis XIV of France and Maria Teresa of Austria, daughter of Philip IV: the Spanish monarch now had two sons, so it would be very difficult for the Spanish throne to fall to French hands; even so, the Spanish King demanded that King Louis XIV sign a clause renouncing the Infanta's rights of succession in exchange for the payment of a dowry that Mazarin initially set at 2 million *escudos*, but which ended up being only 500,000. This sum was never paid, and served as an excuse for Louis XIV to initiate new hostilities in the 'War of Devolution' in 1667.

Collaterally, the question of the Prince de Condé remained unresolved. King Philip IV wanted to be publicly recognised for keeping his promises to his allies, so his diplomats negotiated an honourable exit for Condé with the French; however, members of Philip IV's Council of State urged the sovereign to break his oath with the French Prince, as they felt that the interests of an individual should not take precedence over those of the Monarchy and State. But Philip IV maintained his stubborn defence of Condé and not only for reasons of prestige: if Condé was rehabilitated at the French Court, he would always be grateful to the Spanish monarch, and in case France threatened Spain, the Spanish King would always have the leverage to encourage a rebellion led by Condé. After tense negotiations, Condé obtained a royal pardon and the return of his possessions.[7]

4   A. Domínguez Ortiz, A., *Crisis y Decadencia de la España de los Austrias*, (Barcelona: Ariel, 1973), pp.783–875; Galán, *La Paz de Westfalia*, p.36; J. Lynch, *Los Austrias (1516–1700)* (Barcelona: Crítica, 2000), pp.55–56.

5   To understand the implications of this border better see the numerous works of Oscar Jané Checa, especially his doctoral thesis. *França i Catalunya al Segle XVII. Identitats, Contraidentitats i Ideologies a l'Època Moderna (1640–1700)*, (Barcelona: Universitat Autònoma de Barcelona, 2004). R. J. Valladares Ramírez, 'El Tratado de Paz de los Pirineos: una revisión historiográfica (1888–1988)', in *Espacio, Tiempo y Forma*, Serie IV, Hª Moderna, tome 2, 1989, pp.125–137.

6   Domínguez, *Crisis y Decadencia*, pp.783–875; Galán, *La Paz de Westfalia*, p.36; Lynch, *Los Austrias*, pp.55–55.

7   Amigo, 'La otra imagen', p.190; Galán, *La Paz de Westfalia*, p.36.

The peace treaty also included a general pardon and the restitution of property to all those persecuted during the years of the Catalan uprising of 1640–1659. As for Roussillon, the compromise included maintaining the legal code of the *Usatges* (the Catalan civil code) of Barcelona and its own Catalan institutions north of the Pyrenees, based in Perpignan, but this part of the Treaty was not respected by Louis XIV of France: a year later, the *Usatges* were repealed by the French King, and also the abolition of their own institutions in Roussillon, and the use of the Catalan language was prohibited in the public and official sphere, under penalty of invalidating any document written in a language other than French.[8]

For the historian Israel, the Peace of the Pyrenees was:

> A defeat for the Spanish Crown, in proportions that Philip had tried by all means to avoid since 1648; a defeat that brought with it those consequences that the Madrid Court had most feared: the loss of all Spanish influence within France and on its perimeter; the consolidation of French power in Alsace, Lorraine and the Rhine corridor; and, ultimately, the isolation and mutilation of Spanish power in the Low Countries.[9]

---

8   Domínguez, *Crisis y Decadencia*, p.191; M. Fernández Álvarez, 'El fracaso de la hegemonía española en Europa' in *Historia de España de Ramón Menéndez Pidal* (Madrid: Espasa-Calpe, 1982) t. XXV: La España de Felipe IV, p.785; Galán, *La Paz de Westfalia*, p.35; Lynch, *Los Austrias*, p.556.

9   Israel, 'España y Europa', p.336.

Appendix I

Order of Battle of the French Army at the Battle of Lens, 20 August 1648

Commanded by Monsieur Le Prince de Condé

Right Wing: Monsieur Le Prince de Condé
François Carquot-La-Moussaye
Le Marquis du Four
Isaac-Arnaud de Corbeville
Louis-Marie-Victor d'Aumont, Marquis de Villequier

1st Line:
Les Gardes de Prince de Condé, 1 squadron
Régiment de Cavalerie de Chappes, 2 squadrons
Régiment de Cavalerie de Coudray-Montpensier, 1 squadron
Régiment de Cavalerie de Saarbrück Allemand, 1 squadron
Régiment de Cavalerie de Vidame d'AmiEnsigns, 1 squadron
Régiment de Cavalerie de La Villette, 2 squadrons
Régiment de Cavalerie de Ravenel, 1 squadron

(artillery)

2nd Line: Monsieur de Narmoutier
Régiment de Cavalerie du Son Altesse Royal, 2 Squadrons
Régiment de Cavalerie de La Meilleraye Hongrois, 1 squadron
Régiment de Cavalerie de Streef Weymarien, 1 squadron
Régiment de Cavalerie de Saint-Simon, 1 squadron
Régiment de Cavalerie de Bussy-Almoru, 1 squadron
Régiment de Cavalerie d'Harcourt la Vielle, 1 squadron
Régiment de Cavalerie de Beaujeu, 1 squadron

Centre: Monsieur Gaspard de Châtillon

1st Line
Régiments d'Infanterie de Picardie and de Son Altesse Royal, 1 combined battalion
Régiments d'Infanterie d'Erlach Français and de Perrault, 1 combined battalion
(artillery)
Le Régiment des Gardes Suisse, 1 battalion
(artillery)
Le Régiment des Gardes Françaises, 2 battalions
Le Régiment des Gardes Écossais, 1 battalion
(artillery)
Régiment d'Infanterie de Persan, 1 battalion

2nd line
Les Compagnies des Gendarmes et Chevau Légers de Condé and Schomberg
Les Compagnies des Gendarmes et Chevau Légers de la Reine
Les Compagnies des Gendarmes et Chevau Légers du Roy
Les Compagnies des Chevau Légers d'Enghien and du Roy
Les Compagnies des Gendarmes et Chevau Légers de Conti
Les Compagnies des Gendarmes et Chevau Légers d'Enghien, de Langueville, and de Marsillac

3rd Line
Régiments d'Infanterie de La Reine and Rokeby Anglais, 1 combined battalion
Régiments d'Infanterie d'Erlach Allemand and Rasilly, 1 combined battalion
Régiment d'Infanterie de Mazarin Italien, 1 battalion
Régiment d'Infanterie de Conti, 1 battalion
Régiment d'Infanterie de Condé, 1 battalion

Reserve: Monsieur Jean-Louis d'Erlach
Régiment de Cavalerie de Fabry, 1 squadron
Régiment de Cavalerie d'Erlach Allemand, 3 squadrons
Régiment de Cavalerie de Sirot Hongrois, 1 squadron
Régiment de Cavalerie de Ruvigny, 1 squadron

Left Wing: Monsieur le *Maréchal* Henri, Marquis de La Ferté-Sennectère
    Monsieur le *Maréchal* Antoine de Gramont, Duc de Gramont

1st Line
(artillery)
Régiment de Cavalerie de Beintz Weymarien, 2 squadrons
Régiment de Cavalerie de La Ferté Senectèrre, 2 squadrons
Régiment de Cavalerie de Gramont, 2 squadrons
Régiment de Cavalerie de Cardinal Mazarin, 2 squadrons

Les Gardes de Le Duc de Gramont, Les Gardes du Le Marquis de La Ferté-Sennectère, Régiment de Cavalerie de Carabins d'Arnaud, 1 consolidated squadron

2nd Line: Monsieur Jacques de Rougé, Marquis de Plessis-Bellière
Régiment de Cavalerie de La Roche-Chémerault Croates, 1 squadron
Régiment de Cavalerie de Meille, 1 squadron
Régiment de Cavalerie de Noirlieu, 2 squadrons
Régiment de Cavalerie de Lille-bonne, 1 squadron
Régiment de Cavalerie de Gesvres, 1 squadron
Régiment de Cavalerie de Roquelaure, 1 squadron

Sources:
Le Bataille de Lens en Flandre Gaignée par l'Armée du tres Chrés. Louys XIIII. Roy de France et de Navarre Commandée par Monseig^{eur} Le Prince de Condé sur l'armée Espagnolle Commandée par l'Archiduc Leopold le 20e Jour d'Aoust 1648.

Relation de la Bataille Donnee pres la Ville de lens en Artois…: Paris 1694.

Appendix II

Casualties in the French Army at the Battle of Lens, 20 August 1648

Régiment de Cavalerie de Chappes
    Le Sieur de Fraisiliere, killed
    Le Sieur de Blais, mortally wounded
Régiment de Cavalerie de Saarbrück Allemand
    Le Mestre de Camp Le Comte de Nassau-Saarbrück, killed
    Captain and Major Le Sieur de la Salle, killed
    Le Sieur de Tronquet, mortally wounded
Régiment de Cavalerie de Vidame d'Amiens
    Le Sieur de Catteu, wounded
    Le Sieur de Viue, wounded
Régiment de Cavalerie de La Villette
    Captain and Major Le Sieur du Long, wounded
    Le Sieur Fromy, mortally wounded
    Le Sieur Ditton, wounded
Régiment de Cavalerie de Ravenel
    Le Sieur Iocon, killed
    Le Sieur Bessol, wounded
    Le Sieur Uguerin, wounded
Régiment de Cavalerie du Son Altesse Royal
    Mestre de Camp Le Comte de Brancas, prisoner
    Le Sieur de Motthe Descras, killed
    Le Sieur de Malue, mortally wounded
    Le Sieur de Colincourt, wounded and prisoner
    Le Sieur de Beaupré, prisoner
Régiment de Cavalerie de Streef Weymarien
    Colonel Jean de Streef, wounded
    The Major, killed
    One Captain, wounded
    One Lieutenant, wounded

Régiment de Cavalerie de Saint-Simon
    Le Sieur d'Auteruie, prisoner
Régiment de Cavalerie de Bussy-Almoru
    Captain Le Sieur de Bussy, wounded
    Captain Le Sieur de Jumelle, wounded
Régiment de Cavalerie d'Harcourt la Vielle
    Le Sieur de Colligny, wounded
    Le Sieur du Val, wounded
    Le Sieur de Torigny, wounded
Régiment de Cavalerie de Beaujeu
    Le Sieur de Mesanger, wounded
    Le Sieur d'Arnan, wounded
    Le Sieur de Liuan, wounded
Régiment d'Infanterie de Picardie
    Le Mestre de Camp Le Duc de La Vieuville, wounded
    Le Sieur de Loigny, killed
    Le Sieur de St Leonard, wounded
    Le Sieur de Leschelle, wounded
Régiment d'Infanterie de Son Altesse Royal
    Le Sieur de la Tour, killed
    Le Sieur de Villechaune, mortally wounded
Le Régiment des Gardes Suisse
    Captain Le Sieur Hessy, killed
    Captain Le Sieur Gibelin, killed
    Le Sieur Soury and 7 junior officers, killed
    Lieutenant Le Sieur Vittenbusch, Ensign Le Sieur Escher and 11 junior officers wounded
Le Régiment des Gardes Françaises
    Le Sieur de l'Anglade, wounded
    Le Sieur de Nancré, wounded
    his Lieutenant wounded 'de cinq coups', prisoner,
    his Ensign, killed
    Le Sieur de Villermont, wounded
    Le Sieur de Pontet, prisoner
    Le Sieur Saint Val, killed
    his Lieutenant, killed
    Le Sieur de Bellebrune, wounded
    his Lieutenant, killed
    Le Sieur de Noncourt, killed
    Lieutenant de Lognac, killed
    Le Sieur Renoüard, wounded
    Lieutenant de Dutille, wounded
    Le Sieur de Charmazel, prisoner
    his Lieutenant, prisoner
    his Ensign, prisoner
    Le Sieur de Villiers, wounded
    his Ensign, wounded
    Captain Le Sieur de Boisauid, killed

Captain Le Sieur Boisseleau, wounded
Captain Le Sieur Hervilliers, wounded
Captain Le Sieur Ianlis, wounded
Captain Le Sieur de Pradelles, wounded
Le Sieur de Porcheuse, wounded
Le Sieur de Matarel, wounded
Le Sieur de Riberpré, prisoner
Lieutenant Le Sieurs de Cursy, wounded
Lieutenant Le Sieur de Vieux Bourg, wounded
Le Sieur Hericourt, killed
Le Sieur de Salins, prisoner
Ensign Le Sieur de Brossin, wounded
Ensign Le Sieur de Bozicourt, wounded
Le Sieur de Cavoy, killed

Le Régiment des Gardes Écossais
The Major killed
Le Sieur Makmak, mortally wounded
Captain Le Sieur Lindsay, mortally wounded
Captain Le Sieur de Grome, wounded
Captain Le Sieur Handerson, wounded
Captain Le Sieur Gordon, wounded
Lieutenant Le Sieur Tormniston, wounded
Lieutenant Le Sieur Kinchtbz, wounded
Ensign Le Sieur Stevenel, wounded

La Compagnie des Chevau Legers de Condé
Le Sieur de Guitaut, wounded and prisoner
Le Sieur de Corent, wounded and prisoner

La Compagnie des Gendarmes de la Reine
Lieutenant Le Sieur de Franquetot, wounded

La Compagnie des Gendarmes du Roy
Maréchal de Logis Le Sieur de Cornier, wounded

La Compagnie des Chevau Legers du Roy
Maréchal de Logis Le Sieur de Rhodes, wounded

La Compagnie des Chevau Legers de Conti
Cornet Le Sieur de Montaterr, wounded

La Compagnie des Gendarmes d'Enghien
Lieutenant Le Sieur de Brabantane, wounded

La Compagnie des Chevau Legers d'Enghien
Lieutenant Le Sieur de Beaujeu, killed
Guidon Le Sieur de Tupigny, wounded

La Compagnie des Gendarmes de Langueville
Guidon Le Sieur de Guitteri, prisoner

La Compagnie des Gendarmes de Marsillac
Lieutenant Le Sieur d'Oyse, killed

Régiment de Cavalerie de Fabry
One Lieutenant killed

Régiment de Cavalerie d'Erlach Allemand
One Cornet killed

One Captain wounded

Régiment de Cavalerie de Sirot Hongrois

Lieutenant and Colonel killed

Major Le Sieur Brakat, wounded

Régiment de Cavalerie de Ruvigny

Lieutenant Colonel Streiff, killed

Captain Sieur de Congé, killed

Régiment de Cavalerie de Beintz Weymarien

The Captain and Major, mortally wounded

Le Sieur de Boüis, wounded

Le Sieur du Hamel, wounded

Le Sieur de Sebold, wounded

Régiment de Cavalerie de La Ferté Senectèrre

Le Sieur de Vaubecourt, killed

Le Sieur de la Roise, killed

Le Sieur de Brinon, wounded

Le Sieur de la Vespiere, wounded

Le Sieur d'Offi, wounded

Le Sieur de Morsin, wounded

Régiment de Cavalerie de Gramont

Le Sieur de la Mothe, wounded

Le Sieur de la Garde, wounded

Le Sieur de Moussy, wounded

Le Sieur de Beaugy, wounded

Régiment de Cavalerie de Cardinal Mazarin

Mestre de Camp Le Sieur de Chambor, killed

Le Chevalier d'Obterre, wounded

Le Sieur de Viantez, wounded

Le Sieur d'Erbigny, wounded

Le Sieur de l'Estang, wounded

Régiment de Cavalerie de Noirlieu

Le Sieur de Comble, killed

Le Sieur de Beaufort, mortally wounded

Of the German Brigade

Lieutenant Colonel Polieux, killed

The Lieutenant to the Colonel, killed

Two Captains, wounded

Sources:

Le Bataille de Lens en Flandre Gaignée par l'Armée du tres Chrés. Louys XIIII. Roy de France et de Navarre Commandée par Monseig^{eur} Le Prince de Condé sur l'armée Espagnolle Commandée par l'Archiduc Leopold le 20e Jour d'Aoust 1648.

Relation de la Bataille Donnee pres la Ville de lens en Artois…: Paris 1694.

Appendix III

Order of Battle of the Spanish Army at the Battle of Lens, 20 August 1648[1]

Commanded by the Archduke Leopold William

Right Wing

1st line: Comte de Bucquoy
Unregimented Compañías, 14 squadrons

2nd Line: Prince de Ligne
Unregimented Compañías, 13 squadrons

Centre

1st Line
Caballos Corazas, 4 squadrons 'Escadrons doublees'
Tercio de Ferdinardo Solis
Tercios de Grasse Boniface and de Mr Diassasa, 1 amalgamated battalion
Tercios de Mouroy, de Bec and de La Moterie, 1 amalgamated battalion
Tercios de La Materie and del Grosbandon, 1 amalgamated battalion
Tercio de Vestec
Unregimented Compañías, 4 squadrons
Tercios de Bentinoglio and del Gaspo Italian, 1 amalgamated battalion
Tercio de Touvenin and del Silly (Lorraine), one amalgamated battalion
Caballeria de Luneville (Lorrainer), 2 squadrons
Caballeria de Daygro (Lorraine), 1 squadron

---

1   NB This OoB is taken from a French source so some names will have been rendered in French style. A number of the Spanish infantry units were actually titled as 'Regiment' not as 'Tercio' but the French source gives all as 'Tercio'.

Tercios de Clainmeran (Lorrainer) and del Doumarais Irish, one amalgamated battalion

Tercios de Sirot and de Plonquet Irish, one amalgamated battalion (+Dario ?)

Tercios de Remion (Lorrainer) and de l'Huilier (Lorrainer), one amalgamated battalion

2nd Line
Guardias de Fuensaldagnie, 1 squadron
Guardias de Archduke, 1 squadron
Regimento de Caballeria de Le Fuensaldagne, 1 squadron

3rd Line
Tercio de le Don Baire
Tercio de Don Gabriel de Toledo
Tercio de Borlau
Tercios del Hous and del Chastelein, one amalgamated battalion
Tercio del Mitry
Tercios del Verduisant and del Gondrecourt, one amalgamated battalion

Reserve
Caballos Corazas, 4 squadrons
Caballos, 3 squadrons 'Escadrons doublee' [un-named Regiment]

Left Wing

1st Line: Le Prince de Salm
'Cavalerie de Lorrain'
Caballos del Aigre
Caballos del Montauban
Caballos del Auton, 3 squadrons
Caballos del Catelet, 2 squadrons
Caballos del Volantin, 2 squadrons
Régiment Un-named, 1 squadron

2nd Line: Lieutenant Colonell de Lignoville (Luneville)
'Cavalerie de Lorrain'
Caballos del Baron de Louis, 3 squadrons
Caballos del Melin, 2 squadrons
Caballos del Lignoville, 3 squadrons

Sources:
Le Bataille de Lens en Flandre Gaignée par l'Armée du tres Chrés. Louys XIIII. Roy de France et de Navarre Commandée par Monseig^{eur} Le Prince de Condé sur l'armée Espagnolle Commandée par l'Archiduc Leopold le 20e Jour d'Aoust 1648.

Relation de la Bataille Donnee pres la Ville de lens en Artois…: Paris 1694.

Appendix IV

Prisoners from the Spanish Army at the Battle of Lens[1]

Mestre de Campo Le Baron de Bek, 'General des Armées du Roy d'Espagne and Gov of Luxembourg'
Le Prince de Ligne, General of Cavalry
D. Francisca Albeda, Lieutenant General under the Baron de Bek
Le Comte de Saint Amour
Le Baron de Creuecoeur, *mestre de camp* of infantry and Governor of Avennes
Barnabé de Vergas, *mestre de camp* of infantry
D. Fernando Solis, *mestre de camp*
D. Gabriel de Toledos *mestre de camp* of infantry
Dom Michel de Luna, *Intendant* of the Army
D. Arias Gonsals son to Comte de Punnoincostro
Marquis de Saint Martin, volunteer in the Army of Lorraine
Baron de Beaufort, son of General Bek
D. Antonio Fernandes Cantades, Major of a Spanish regiment
Colonel Housse of the cavalry of Lorraine
Dom Antonio Hurtado de Mendossa, Captain of the Guard of the Archduke and Captain of Guet
Lieutenant Colonel Verduisan of the troops of Lorraine
Lieutenant Colonel Gustin of the troops of Lorraine
Le Sieur Limosin, Lieutenant Colonel of Regiment of D. Joan Mauroy
D. Gaspard Boniface, Colonel of Infantry, Spanish
Le Sieur Galand ADC to Prince de Ligne
Baron de Bonniere, *Mestre de Camp* reformado and Governor of Bethune
D. Francisco de Solis, Adjutant[2] to D. Fernando de Solis
D. Joseph Pons, Adjutant to *Mestre de Camp Général*
D. Michel, Adjutant to General Bek
Le Sieur Masson, *Escuyer* [lit. squire] of the Comte de Saint Amour

---

1   NB This list is taken from a French source so some names will have been rendered in French style. Similarly ranks in the original are given in French, but here have been translated.

2   Although the original says "adj" it may be that a better word would have been "aide", although it has been left as adjutant here.

Bentivoglio, Italian
10 captains, 10 ensigns, 10 ensigns reformado, 6 sergeants, 13 sergeants reformado

D. Jospeh Gouasco, Italian
Mestre de Campo Don Joseph Gouasco,
1 captain, 1 adjutant, 3 ensigns, 3 ensigns reformado, 3 sergeants

Tercio de Bek
4 captains, 5 lieutenants, 4 ensigns, 7 sergeants

D. Gabriel de Toledo, Spanish
1 captain, 5 captains reformado, 11 lieutenants, 27 ensigns reformado, 9 sergeants, 13 sergeants reformado

Barnabé de Barques, Spanish
5 captains, 5 captains reformado, 8 ensigns, 42 ensigns reformado, 10 sergeants, 36 sergeants reformado

Clinchcamp, Lorraine
7 captains, 2 lieutenants, 5 ensigns

Gondrecourt, Lorraine
1 captain, 2 lieutenants, 6 ensigns, 3 sergeants

Chastelain, Lorraine
3 captains, 1 lieutenant, 2 ensigns

l'Huilier, Lorraine
7 captains, 4 lieutenants, 4 ensigns, 1 sergeant

Verduisant, Lorraine
1 captain, 1 adjutant, 2 lieutenants, 1 ensign, 2 sergeants

Mitry, German
5 captains, 1 *auditeur*, 7 lieutenants, 4 ensigns, 1 sergeants

Hous, German
2 captains, 4 lieutenants, 1 ensign, 1 sergeant

Remion, Lorraine
2 captains, 1 lieutenant, 2 ensigns, 1 sergeant

Tercio del Silly, Lorraine
3 captains, 5 lieutenants, 3 ensigns, 4 sergeants

Touvenin, Lorraine
4 lieutenants, 2 ensigns

Desmarets, Irish
8 lieutenants, 3 ensigns

Plonquet, Irish
Lieutenant Colonel Plonquet, 3 captains, 5 lieutenants, 5 ensigns

Sinot, Irish
2 captains, 2 lieutenants, 6 ensigns

D. Fernando de Solis, Spanish
8 captains, 3 captains reformado, 13 ensigns, 48 ensigns reformado, 11 sergeants

Boniface, Spanish
8 captains, 11 ensigns, 55 ensigns reformado, 11 sergeants, 3 sergeants reformado

D. Franscisco Desa, Spanish
4 captains, 5 captains reformado, 26 ensigns, 31 ensigns reformado, 13 sergeants

Guillame Anselme, English
6 captains

D. Jean de Mouroy, 'High Germans'
D. Jean de Mouror, *Mestre de Camp*, 7 captains, 7 lieutenants 15 ensigns, 2 ensigns reformado, 3 sergeants *principaux*, 9 *petits* sergeants

Baron de Wang
1 captain, 3 captains reformado, 3 ensigns

de la Motterie, Walloon
2 captains, 3 captains reformado, 3 ensigns

Comte de Broé, Walloon
8 lieutenants

Comte de Grosbandon, Walloon
4 captains, 13 ensigns

Baron de Creuecoeur, Walloon
5 captains, 5 ensigns

Berlau, German
Lieutenant Colonel Massillon, 3 captains, 3 lieutenants, 8 ensigns, 7 sergeants

Fernand Darias, German
1 captain, 3 lieutenants, 3 ensigns

de Vargue, Spanish
2 captains

Regiment of Infantry, Italian
12 officers of D. Joseph, 7 gentlemen of artillery, 16 *letteurs de feux d'artifices* [fireworks] and volunteers

Sources:
Le Bataille de Lens en Flandre Gaignée par l'Armée du tres Chrés. Louys XIIII. Roy de France et de Navarre Commandée par Monseig^{eur} Le Prince de Condé sur l'armée Espagnolle Commandée par l'Archiduc Leopold le 20e Jour d'Aoust 1648.

Relation de la Bataille Donnee pres la Ville de lens en Artois…: Paris 1694.

Bibliography

Primary Sources

Anonymous, Biblioteca Nacional Hispánica, Mss. 2379, 'Sucesos de Año 1648' (undated, probably 1648 or 1649 but before 1700)

Abreu Y Bertodano, J. A. De, *Colección de los tratados de paz [...]. Reinado de Phelipe IV,* Parte IV (Madrid, Antonio Marín, Juan de Zúñiga y la viuda de Peralta, 1751)

AGS, Estado, leg. 2256, s.f., Felipe IV a Fuensaldaña, 8-XII-1648.

Les Batailles Memorables des François, tome II (Paris: Mabre Cramoisy, 1696)

Beaulieu Sieur de Beaulieu, Sébastien de Pontault, *Les Glorieuses Conquêtes de Louis le Grand, Roy de France et de Navarre* (Paris, 1694), tome 1

Documents relatifs à la bataille de Lens. Gallica. Available on-line at: https://gallica.bnf.fr/ark:/12148/btv1b90594033.r=documents%20 relatifs%20bataille%20lens?rk=21459;2

Mazarin, Jules, *Lettres du Cardinal Mazarin Pendant son Ministère,* tome 3 (Paris: Imprimerie Nationale, 1883)

Pérez, De Vivero Y Menchaca, Alonso, Conde de Fuensaldaña: 'Relación de lo sucedido en Flandes desde 1648 a 1653' in *Colección de Documentos Inéditos para la Historia de España* (CODOIN), tome 75 (Madrid: Miguel Ginesta, 1880), pp.549–576

Prontuario de los Tratados de Paz de España. Reynado de Phelipe IV. Parte IV, V, VI y VII última, pp.82–258 & 299–606. Disponible en la red a través del siguiente enlace: https://books.google.es/books?id=8ZlJAAAAcAAJ&pg=RA1PA383&dq =Tratados+de+paz&hl=es&sa=X&ei=PwDrVIaTFYTvUPHPg_AF&ved =0CFIQ6wEwCQ#v=onepage&q=Tratados%20de%20paz&f=false

Vincart, Juan Antonio, 'Relación de la campaña de 1650' in *Colección de Documentos Inéditos para la Historia de España* (CODOIN), tome 75 (Madrid: Miguel Ginesta, 1880) pp.487–546

Secondary Sources

Printed Books

Aumale, H. d'Orleans, Duc de, *Histoire des Princes de Condé aux XVe et XVIIe Siècles,* tomes 6 & 7, (Paris: Calmann Lévy, 1892–1896)

Béguin, Katia, *Les Princes de Condé. Rebelles, Courtisans et Mécènes dans la France du Grand Siècle* (Seyssel: Champ Vallon, 1999)

Bertière, Simone, *Condé, le Héros Fourvoyé* (Paris: Éditions de Fallois, 2011)

Cánovas del Castillo, Antonio, *Obras Completas,* (Madrid: Fundación Cánovas del Castillo, 1997)

Clodfelter, Micheal, *Warfare and Armed Conflicts: A Statistical Encyclopedia of Casualty and Other Figures, 1492–2015,* (Jefferson: McFarland, 2017)

Cousin, M. Víctor, *La Société Française au XVIIe Siècle, d'Après le Grand Cyrus de Mlle de Scudéry,* (Paris: Didier, 1858)

Desormeaux, M., *Histoire de Louis de Bourbon, second du nom, Prince de Condé,* tome 1 (Paris: Chez Saillant, 1766)

Elliott, J. H., *The Revolt of the Catalans: A Study in the Decline of Spain (1598–1640)* (Cambridge: CUP, 1984)

Esteban Ribas, Alberto Raúl, *La Batalla de Tuttlingen, 1643,* (Madrid: Almena, 2014)

Esteban Ribas, Alberto Raúl, *The Battle of Nördlingen 1634* (Warwick: Helion & Company, 2021)

Estaban Ribas, Alberto Raúl, *The Battle of Rocroi 1643* (Warwick: Helion & Company, 2022)

Galán, Martin, A., *La Paz de Westfalia (1648) y el Nuevo Orden Internacional* (Badajoz: Universidad de Extremadura, 2015)

Godley, Eveline, *The Great Condé: A Life of Louis II De Bourbon, Prince of Condé,* (London: John Murray, 1915)

González de León, Fernando, *The Road to Rocroi Class, Culture and Command in the Spanish Army of Flanders, 1567–1659.* (Leiden: Brill, 2009)

Goulas, Nicolas, *Memoires de Nicolas Goulas,* tome II (Paris: Renouard, 1879)

Guthrie, William P., *Batallas de la Guerra de los Treinta Años. Segundo Período* (Madrid: Ediciones Salamina, 2017)

Hardy de Perini, Général, *Batailles Françaises, tome IV: Turenne et Condé, 1643 à 1671* (Paris: Ernest Flammarion, 1906)

Harrington, M. C, *The Worke Wee May Doe in the World. The Western Design and the Anglo-Spanish Struggle for the Caribbean, 1654–1655* (Tallahassee: Florida State University, 2004)

Inglish-Jones, James John, *The Grand Condé in exile: Power Politics in France, Spain and the Spanish Netherlands. 1652–1659* (Oxford: OUP, 1994)

Jané Checa, Oscar, *França i Catalunya al Segle XVII. Identitats, Contraidentitats i Ideologies a l'Època Moderna (1640–1700)* (Bellaterra: Universitat Autònoma de Barcelona, 2004)

Lafuente, Modesto, *Historia General de España,* tome XII (Barcelone: Montaner y Simón, 1889)

Lonchay, Henri, *Correspondance de la Cour d'Espagne sur les Affaires des Pays-Bas au XVIIe siècle,* volume 4 (Bruxelles: Maurice Lamertin, 1933)

Lonchay, Henri, *La Rivalité de la France et de l'Espagne aux Pays-Bas (1635–1700),* (Bruxelles: Hayez, 1896)

Lynch J., *Los Austrias (1516–1700)* (Barcelona: Crítica, 2000)

Maffi, Davide, *En Defensa del Imperio. Los Ejércitos de Felipe IV y la Guerra por la Hegemonía Europea (1635–1659)* (Madrid: Actas, 2014)

Malo, Charles, *Champs de Bataille de France* (Paris: Hachette, 1899)

Montglat, Marquis de, *Collection des Mémoires Relatifs à l'Histoire de France* (Paris: Foucault, 1826)

Pestana, C. G., *The English Conquest of Jamaica: Oliver Cromwell's Bid for Empire* (Harvard: Harvard University Press, 2017)

Pujo, B., *Le Grand Condé,* Albin Michel, Paris, 1995.

Quincy, Marquis de, *Histoire Militaire du Regne de Louis Le Grand,* (Paris: Jean-Baptiste Delespine, 1726)

Sanz Camañes, Porfirio, *Tiempo de Cambios. Guerra, Diplomacia y Política Internacional de la Monarquía Hispánica (1648–1700)* (Madrid: Actas, 2013)

Sanabre, Josep, *La Acción de Francia en Cataluña en la Pugna por la Hegemonía de Europa, 1640–1659* (Barcelona: J. Sala Badal, 1956)

Sicilia Cardona, Enrique F., *La Guerra de Portugal (1640–1668)* (Madrid: Actas, 2022)

Thion, Stéphane, *Les Armées Françaises de la Guerre de Trente Ans* (Auzielle: LRT Éditions, 2008)

Wilson, Peter H., *Europe's Tragedy: A New History of the Thirty Years' War* (London: Penguin, 2010)

Printed Articles and Chapters

Alcalá-Zamora Y Queipo De Llano, J., 'La Monarquía Hispánica y la fase final de la Guerra de Flandes', en *El Final de la Guerra de Flandes (1621–1648). 350 Aniversario de la Paz de Münster* (Madrid: Fundación Carlos Amberes, 1998) pp.17–25

Amigo Vázquez, Lourdes, 'Un Nuevo Escenario de la Guerra con Francia. La intervención española en la Fronda (1648–1653)' in *Stud. his., H.ᵃ mod.,* 41, n.1 (2019), pp.153–188

Amigo Vázquez, Lourdes, 'La otra imagen del héroe. El Grand Condé como aliado del rey de España (1651–1659)' in *Investigaciones Históricas, época moderna y contemporánea,* 38 (2018), pp.187–218.

Black, C., *The Story of Jamaica from Prehistory to the Present* (London: Collins, 1965) pp.46–50

Domínguez Ortiz, A., *Crisis y Decadencia de la España de los Austrias,* (Barcelona: Ariel, 1973)

Duchhardt, H., 'La Paz de Westfalia como *lieu de mémoire* en Alemania y Europa', in *Pedralbes,* 19 (1999), pp.147–155.

Elliott, J. H., 'Europa Después de la Paz de Westfalia', *Pedralbes,* 19 (1999), pp.131–146.

Fernández Álvarez, M., 'El fracaso de la hegemonía española en Europa' in *Historia de España de Ramón Menéndez Pidal* (Madrid: Espasa-Calpe, 1982) t. XXV: La España de Felipe IV, pp.635–789.

García, B. J., 'La guerra de los Treinta Años y otros conflictos asociados', in *Historia Moderna Universal* (Barcelona: Ariel Historia, 2002), pp.383–409.

García, B. J., 'La Paz de Münster: un nuevo horizonte', in *El final de la guerra de Flandes (1621–1648). 350 Aniversario de la Paz de Münster* (Madrid: Fundación Carlos Amberes, 1998), pp.159–172.

Inglish-Jones, James John, 'The Battle of the Dunes, 1658: Condé, War and Power Politics' in *War in History*, 1–3 (1994), pp.249–277

Israel, J., 'España y Europa. Desde el Tratado de Münster a la Paz de los Pirineos, 1648–1659' in *Pedralbes*, 29 (2009), pp.271–337

Janicki, J., 'La puissance espagnole est anéantie en 1648 à la Bataille de Lens' in *L'Avenir de l'Artois,* édition internet, 2009

Manzano Baena, L., 'El largo camino hacia la paz. Cambios y semejanzas entre la Tregua de Amberes de 1609 y la Paz de Münster de 1648' in *Pedralbes*, 29 (2009), pp.159–194

Rodríguez González, A. R., 'Un afortunado golpe de mano anfibio: Burdeos, 20 de Octubre de 1653' in *Revista General de Marina,* 2018, 12, pp.879–885.

Schmidt, P., 'La Paz de Westfalia' in *Historia de Europa a Través de sus Documentos* (Barcelona: Lunwerg, 2012), pp.105–119

Valladares Ramírez, R. J., 'El Tratado de Paz de los Pirineos: una revisión historiográfica (1888–1988)' in *Espacio, Tiempo y Forma*, Serie IV, Hª Moderna, Tome 2, 1989, pp.125–137

Valladares Ramírez, R. J., *La Rebelión de Portugal: guerra, conflicto y poderes en la monarquía hispánica (1640–1680)* (Valladolid: Junta de Castilla y León, 1998), pp.142–144

Vermeir, R., 'Un Austriaco en Flandes. El Archiduque Leopoldo Guillermo, Gobernador General de los Países Bajos meridionales (1647–1656)' in *La Dinastía de los Austria: las relaciones entre la Monarquía Católica y el Imperio* (Madrid: Ediciones Polifemo, 2011), Volume 1, pp.583–608

Yetano Laguna, I., *Relaciones Entre España y Francia desde la paz de los Pirineos (1659) hasta la guerra de devolución (1667). La embajada del Marqués de la Fuente* (Madrid: Uned, 2007), pp.21–47

About the Author

Alberto Raúl Esteban Ribas is a Spanish historian and economist. He is studying a doctorate in Military History. He is a specialist in the military history of Spain of the sixteenth and seventeenth centuries. He has written several books on Spanish battles and military expeditions, as well as numerous articles for Spanish and international magazines. His current line of research focuses on the study of the Spanish armies and campaigns of the second half of the seventeenth century, considered the period of Spanish decline, and analysing the reasons for such a situation.

About the Artists

Sergey Shamenkov graduated from the Academy of Arts in Lviv, and he now lives and works in Odessa, Ukraine. He is an author of articles, books, and of scientific graphic reconstructions on the subject of clothing, material and military culture of the Ukrainian Cossacks, material and military culture of the Polish-Lithuanian Commonwealth, as well as of the Army of Sweden, and of other European armies, for Helion and other publishers. He has also illustrated a number of books published by Helion & Co.

Giorgio Albertini was born in 1968 in Milan where he still lives. After studying Medieval History at the University of Milan, he become involved in archaeology and has been involved in several excavations for European institutions. He was responsible for the graphic depiction of archaeological sites and finds. He also works as a historical and scientific illustrator for many institutions, museums, and magazines such as *National Geographic Magazine*, *BBC History*, and *Medieval Warfare*. He has always been interested in military history and is one of the founders of *Focus Wars* magazine.

Other titles in the Century of the Soldier series

No 37 *William III's Italian Ally: Piedmont and the War of the League of Augsburg 1683-1697*

No 38 *Wars and Soldiers in the Early Reign of Louis XIV: Volume 1 - The Army of the United Provinces of the Netherlands, 1660-1687*

No 39 *In The Emperor's Service: Wallenstein's Army, 1625-1634*

No 40 *Charles XI's War: The Scanian War Between Sweden and Denmark, 1675-1679*

No 41 *The Armies and Wars of The Sun King 1643-1715: Volume 1: The Guard of Louis XIV*

No 42 *The Armies Of Philip IV Of Spain 1621-1665: The Fight For European Supremacy*

No 43 *Marlborough's Other Army: The British Army and the Campaigns of the First Peninsular War, 1702-1712*

No 44 *The Last Spanish Armada: Britain And The War Of The Quadruple Alliance, 1718-1720*

No 45 *Essential Agony: The Battle of Dunbar 1650*

No 46 *The Campaigns of Sir William Waller*

No 47 *Wars and Soldiers in the Early Reign of Louis XIV: Volume 2 - The Imperial Army, 1660-1689*

No 48 *The Saxon Mars and His Force: The Saxon Army During The Reign Of John George III 1680-1691*

No 49 *The King's Irish: The Royalist Anglo-Irish Foot of the English Civil War*

No 50 *The Armies and Wars of the Sun King 1643-1715: Volume 2: The Infantry of Louis XIV*

No 51 *More Like Lions Than Men: Sir William Brereton and the Cheshire Army of Parliament, 1642-46*

No 52 *I Am Minded to Rise: The Clothing, Weapons and Accoutrements of the Jacobites from 1689 to 1719*

No 53 *The Perfection of Military Discipline: The Plug Bayonet and the English Army 1660-1705*

No 54 *The Lion From the North: The Swedish Army During the Thirty Years War: Volume 1, 1618-1632*

No 55 *Wars and Soldiers in the Early Reign of Louis XIV: Volume 3 - The Armies of the Ottoman Empire 1645-1718*

No 56 *St. Ruth's Fatal Gamble: The Battle of Aughrim 1691 and the Fall Of Jacobite Ireland*

No 57 *Fighting for Liberty: Argyll & Monmouth's Military Campaigns against the Government of King James, 1685*

No 58 *The Armies and Wars of the Sun King 1643-1715: Volume 3: The Cavalry of Louis XIV*

No 59 *The Lion From the North: The Swedish Army During the Thirty Years War: Volume 2, 1632-1648*

No 60 *By Defeating My Enemies: Charles XII of Sweden and the Great Northern War 1682-1721*

No 61 *Despite Destruction, Misery and Privations..: The Polish Army in Prussia during the war against Sweden 1626-1629*

No 62 *The Armies of Sir Ralph Hopton: The Royalist Armies of the West 1642-46*

No 63 *Italy, Piedmont, and the War of the Spanish Succession 1701-1712*

No 64 *'Cannon played from the great fort': Sieges in the Severn Valley during the English Civil War 1642-1646*

No 65 *Carl Gustav Armfelt and the Struggle for Finland During the Great Northern War*

No 66 *In the Midst of the Kingdom: The Royalist War Effort in the North Midlands 1642-1646*

No 67 *The Anglo-Spanish War 1655-1660: Volume 1: The War in the West Indies*

No 68 *For a Parliament Freely Chosen: The Rebellion of Sir George Booth, 1659*

No 69 *The Bavarian Army During the Thirty Years War 1618-1648: The Backbone of the Catholic League (revised second edition)*

No 70 *The Armies and Wars of the Sun King 1643-1715: Volume 4: The War of the Spanish Succession, Artillery, Engineers and Militias*

No 71 *No Armour But Courage: Colonel Sir George Lisle, 1615-1648 (Paperback reprint)*

No 72 *The New Knights: The Development of Cavalry in Western Europe, 1562-1700*

No 73 *Cavalier Capital: Oxford in the English Civil War 1642-1646 (Paperback reprint)*

No 74 *The Anglo-Spanish War 1655-1660: Volume 2: War in Jamaica*

No 75 *The Perfect Militia: The Stuart Trained Bands of England and Wales 1603-1642*

No 76 *Wars and Soldiers in the Early Reign of Louis XIV: Volume 4 - The Armies of Spain 1659-1688*

No 77 *The Battle of Nördlingen 1634: The Bloody Fight Between Tercios and Brigades*

No 78 *Wars and Soldiers in the Early Reign of Louis XIV: Volume 5 - The Portuguese Army 1659-1690*

No 79 *We Came, We Saw, God Conquered: The Polish-Lithuanian Commonwealth's military effort in the relief of Vienna, 1683*

No 80 *Charles X's Wars: Volume 1 - Armies of the Swedish Deluge, 1655-1660*

No 81 *Cromwell's Buffoon: The Life and Career of the Regicide, Thomas Pride (Paperback reprint)*

No 82 *The Colonial Ironsides: English Expeditions under the Commonwealth and Protectorate, 1650-1660*

No 83 *The English Garrison of Tangier: Charles II's Colonial Venture in the Mediterranean, 1661-1684*

No 84 *The Second Battle of Preston, 1715: The Last Battle on English Soil*

No 85 *To Settle the Crown: Waging Civil War in Shropshire, 1642-1648 (Paperback reprint)*

No 86 *A Very Gallant Gentleman: Colonel Francis Thornhagh (1617-1648) and the Nottinghamshire Horse*

No 87 *Charles X's Wars: Volume 2 - The Wars in the East, 1655-1657*

No 88 *The Shōgun's Soldiers: The Daily Life of Samurai and Soldiers in Edo Period Japan, 1603-1721 Volume 1*

No 89 *Campaigns of the Eastern Association: The Rise of Oliver Cromwell, 1642-1645*

No 90 *The Army of Occupation in Ireland 1603-42: Defending the Protestant Hegemony*

No 91 *The Armies and Wars of the Sun King 1643-1715: Volume 5: Buccaneers and Soldiers in the Americas*

No 92 *New Worlds, Old Wars: The Anglo-American Indian Wars 1607-1678*

No 93 *Against the Deluge: Polish and Lithuanian Armies During the War Against Sweden 1655-1660*

No 94 *The Battle of Rocroi: The Battle, the Myth and the Success of Propaganda*

No 95 *The Shōgun's Soldiers: The Daily Life of Samurai and Soldiers in Edo Period Japan, 1603-1721 Volume 2*

No 96 *Science of Arms: the Art of War in the Century of the Soldier 1672-1699: Volume 1: Preparation for War and the Infantry*

No 97 *Charles X's Wars: Volume 3 - The Danish Wars 1657-1660*

No 98 *Wars and Soldiers in the Early Reign of Louis XIV: Volume 6 - Armies of the Italian States 1660-1690 Part 1*

No 99 *Dragoons and Dragoon Operations in the British Civil Wars, 1638-1653*

No 100 *Wars and Soldiers in the Early Reign of Louis XIV: Volume 6 - Armies of the Italian States 1660-1690 Part 2*

No 101 *1648 and All That: The Scottish Invasions of England, 1648 and 1651: Proceedings of the 2022 Helion and Company 'Century of the Soldier' Conference*

No 102 *John Hampden and the Battle of Chalgrove:*

The Political and Military Life of Hampden and his Legacy

No 103 *The City Horse: London's militia cavalry during the English Civil War, 1642-1660*

No 104 *The Battle of Lützen 1632: A Reassessment*

No 105 *Monmouth's First Rebellion: The Later Covenanter Risings, 1660-1685*

No 106 *Raw Generals and Green Soldiers: Catholic Armies in Ireland 1641-1643*

No 107 *Polish, Lithuanian and Cossack armies versus the might of the Ottoman Empire*

No 108 *Soldiers and Civilians, Transport and Provisions: Early Modern Military Logistics and Supply Systems During The British Civil Wars, 1638-1653*

No 109 *Batter their walls, gates and Forts: The Proceedings of the 2022 English Civil War Fortress Symposium*

No 110 *The Town Well Fortified: The Fortresses of the Civil Wars in Britain, 1639-1660*

No 111 *Crucible of the Jacobite '15: The Battle of Sheriffmuir 1715*

No 112 *Charles XII's Karoliners Volume 2 - The Swedish Cavalry of the Great Northern War 1700-1721*

No 113 *Wars and Soldiers in the Early Reign of Louis XIV: Volume 7 - Armies of the German States 1655-1690 Part 1*

No 114 *The First British Army 1624-1628: The Army of the Duke of Buckingham (Revised Edition)*

No 115 *The Army of Transylvania (1613-1690): War and military organization from the 'golden age' of the Principality to the Habsburg conquest*

No 116 *The Army of the Manchu Empire: The Conquest Army and the Imperial Army of Qing China, 1600-1727*

No 117 *French Armies of The Thirty Years' War 1618-48*

No 118 *Soldiers' Clothing of the Early 17th Century: Britain and Western Europe 1618-1660*

No 119 *Novelty and Change: Proceedings of the 2023 Helion and ompany 'Century of the Soldier' Conference*

No 120 *Peter The Great's Disastrous Defeat: The Swedish Victory at Narva, 1700*

No 121 *Royalist Newark 1642-1646: Sieges and Siege Works*

No 122 *The Battle of Fribourg 1644: Eughien and Turenne at War*

No 123 *Science of Arms: the Art of War in the Century of the Soldier 1672-1699: Volume 2: Cavalry, Artillery & the Conduct of War*

No 124 *Supplying the New Model Army: Logistics, arms, ammunition, clothing, victuals and the matériel of war, 1645-1646*

No 125 *Wars and Soldiers in the Early Reign of Louis XIV: Volume 7 - Armies of the German States 1655-1690 Part 2*

No 126 *Wars and Soldiers in the Early Reign of Louis XIV: Volume 7 - Armies of the German States 1655-1690 Part 3*

No 127 *Confrontation of Kings, 1656: The Three-Day Battle of Warsaw in the Swedish Deluge, 1655-1660*

No 128 *The Battle of Lens: Condé beats the Spanish*

SERIES SPECIALS:

No 1 *Charles XII's Karoliners: Volume 1: The Swedish Infantry & Artillery of the Great Northern War 1700-1721*